SAME OLD MOON

Same Old Moon had its premiere at Ireland's Druid Theatre in 1984. Garry Hynes directed Jane Brennan, Marie Mullen, Sean McGinley, Ray McBride, Mary Ryan, Mairead Noone, Rebecca Bartlett and Pauline McLynn in a production designed by Monica Frawley with lighting by Barbara Bradshaw.

A revised production was staged at the Oxford Playhouse on 18th April 1991. The play was subsequently presented at the Globe Theatre, London, by The Theatre Division on 3rd May 1991 with the following cast:

Desmond	James Ellis
Bridie/Granny Cleary	Britta Smith
Brenda	Gabrielle Reidy
Peace/Mrs Brown	Eileen Nicholas
Bella/Di/Nurse	Clare Cathcart
Mother Superior/Café Daphne/ Mrs Geeny	Joan Sheehy
Mooney/Michael the Postman/ Caruso/Mr Mullen	Tony Guilfoyle
Mark/Kevin/Priest/ Trevor/Bartender	J. D. Kelleher

Directed by **Jenny Killick**
Designed by **Joe Vanek**
Lighting by **Mick Hughes**
Choreography by **Terry John Bates**

The play is set in London, Dublin and Galway, and takes place between the 1940s and 1980s

Same Old Moon

A play

Geraldine Aron

Samuel French - London
New York - Toronto - Hollywood

SYNOPSIS OF SCENES

Prologue

ACT I	SCENE 1	1980s.	Living room and bedroom of a small London flat
	SCENE 2	1941.	A Dublin pub
	SCENE 3	1950.	Bedroom of Dublin house
	SCENE 4	1950.	Office of a convent school
	SCENE 5	1951.	Bedroom of a Galway house
	SCENE 6	1953.	Kitchen of a scruffy café
	SCENE 7	1953.	Kitchen of a Galway house
	SCENE 8	1953.	A street in Galway
ACT II	SCENE 1	1953.	A street in London
	SCENE 2	1953.	Playground of Rest Centre
	SCENE 3	1956.	Epsom racecourse
	SCENE 4	1961.	London bedsitter
	SCENE 5	1962.	The London flat
	SCENE 6	1962.	On board a ship
	SCENE 7	1965.	The London flat
	SCENE 8	1968.	On board a ship
	SCENE 9	1968.	The London flat
	SCENE 10	1976.	A hospital ward
	SCENE 11	1980s.	The London flat

CHARACTERS

Brenda
Desmond
Peace
Bridie
Bartender
Mooney
Mother Superior
Bella Rafferty
Granny Cleary
Priest
Café Daphne
The Voice of Enrico Caruso
Michael the Postman
Kevin
Mr Mullen
Mrs Geeny
Mrs Brown
Di
Trevor
Mark
Nurse

A company wishing to reduce the size of the cast may divide the roles between five women and three men, as follows:

Women

1 Brenda—nine to forty+
2 Bridie—thirty-eight to sixty-eight. Granny Cleary—eighty
3 Peace—thirty-three to sixty-two. Mrs Brown—fifty
4 Bella—seventeen. Di—twelve and twenty. Nurse—twenty
5 Mother Superior. Café Daphne. Mrs Geeny. All mature.

Men

1 Desmond—thirty to sixty-six
2 Mooney, Michael, Caruso, Mullen. All 40+
3 Priest—twenty. Kevin—twenty. Trevor—twelve. Mark—twenty-four and twenty-eight
   Bartender—thirty

CHARACTERS

Brenda. Age nine to forty. Accents: Western Irish, London and well-spoken London. Perhaps reddish hair.

Peace. Thirties to sixties. Brenda's aunt. Full of anger and resentment. Wears glasses at all ages. Literate Irish accent. (Galway if possible)

Bridie. Thirties to sixties. Brenda's mother. Gentler than her sister Peace, lovely when young and always well groomed.

Desmond. Thirties to sixties. Brenda's father. Preferably red haired. Less cultured than Bridie's family. A charming but destructive Dubliner.

Bartender. Dublin man. Thirtyish.

Mooney. Forties. A Dublin acquaintance of Desmond's.

Mother Superior. A stout Dominican nun. Galway accent if possible.

Bella Rafferty. Seventeen. The town tart. Big, brazen and full of herself. Able to dance.

Granny Cleary. Brenda's Granny. A truly ancient version of Bridie.

Priest. Brenda's fantasy. Handsome, sexy and super cool. Able to dance.

Café Daphne. Forties. Colourful and vulgar. Galway accent if possible.

The Voice of Enrico Caruso. Fortyish. A make-believe Italian tenor, who is actually an Irishman. Able to sing.

Postman. Forty. Galway man. Very inquisitive.

Kevin. Twenty. Brenda's shy, melancholy cousin from Dublin. A quiet, simple young man.

Mr Mullen. Forty. A rough, scruffy Dubliner.

Mrs Geeny and **Mrs Brown.** Fifties. A pair of cold-as-charity social workers. Specs on chains, stout shoes, WVS types.

Di. At twelve she's a violent cockney urchin, skilled at walking on stilts. At twenty she's a nifty dresser. Able to dance.

Trevor. Another cockney urchin, aged twelve. Skilled at stilt-walking.

Mark. Twenty-four and twenty-eight. Brenda's boyfriend and husband. Rather formal, conservative and well spoken. Able to dance.

Nurse. Twenties. Crisp and competent.

SUGGESTIONS FOR STAGING AND COSTUMING

Same Old Moon can be staged with minimal sets, moved on and off swiftly so that there's no loss of pace between the scenes. As one scene ends, actors can strike their furniture and props, sometimes while delivering lines, and while items for the next scene are brought on. Thus the scene changing becomes an integral part of the play. Where possible, items such as a picture, a laundry rack, a statue, etc can be flown in. When this convention is used, a group of key artefacts should remain DL throughout the play, making it clear that Brenda is reviewing her life.

Because Brenda appears in almost every scene, playing nine to forty-plus, a good costume for her might be a simple navy pleated skirt and a well cut white shirt. This can be accessorised as required, with a jacket, a school blazer, a jumper worn on or around the shoulders, scarves, hair bands etc. Her footwear can be changed as needed to show the passing of the years. A classic bob works well for her hair, which ideally would be the same colour as Desmond's hair.

The other players' costumes should be appropriate to their life and times.

The Explorer
By Brenda Barnes Aged 9
Rosary Convent, Galway, Eire, Europe,
Earth, the Wold, The Universe.

This man Called ~~went~~ Conrad wanted to
Explore the world to see would he have a
more ~~gas~~ enjoyable life in another Place Than The Place
he was in.
He got a boat and rowed off. He went very
fast in the begining But then his arms
went week and he had to slow down.
When he had seen everything He Rowed
home and said to his wife in a very
annoyed voice. "Dorathy" he said "I may
as well have stayed where I was because
no matter ~~wh~~ how far I went in the boat
I could not get Away from the same
Old moon."
The End.

poor spelling

$\frac{4}{10}$

For Bill and Sheila Fahy
Garry Hynes and Ned Sherrin.
With love and thanks.

PROLOGUE

1980s

The stage is empty except for a group of artefacts DL. *There is a stool, a small statue of the Blessed Virgin Mary, an old teddy-bear or doll, a school exercise book, brown school sandals and a pair of white socks*

As the CURTAIN *rises we hear a gentle passage from the Mozart theme music, which continues softly throughout the scene*

Brenda enters slowly, carrying her suitcase and briefcase. She is wearing a fur coat. She goes to the stool, puts down her luggage, picks up the exercise book and reads its front cover

Brenda (*cheerfully*) "Brenda Barnes, aged nine, Rosary Convent, Galway, Ireland, Europe, Earth, the World, the Universe ..." (*She smiles, pages through the book, then stops at an essay*) "The Explorer. This man called Conrad wanted to explore the world to see would he have a more enjoyable life in another place than the place he was in. He got a boat and rowed off. He went very fast in the beginning but then his arms went weak and he had to slow down. When he had seen everything he rowed home and said to his wife in a very annoyed voice: "Dorothy," he said, "I might as well have stayed where I was, because no matter how far I rowed in the boat, I could not get away from the same old moon."

The theme music continues. Brenda puts down the essay book and picks up her luggage

Brenda exits slowly as:

The Actors for Scene 1 enter bringing on the furniture for the scene

ACT I

Scene 1

1980s. The Homecoming Scene. The living room and bedroom of a small, cramped flat in London

When completely set, the living room should feature a two-seater sofa, an easy chair, a small table, a radio. We hear the sound of squabbling birds

In the bedroom section, the dimly lit ghost of Desmond, wearing pyjamas and looking middle-aged, sits up in bed, a folded newspaper to hand. He reacts from time to time but is generally still and inconspicuous

Peace enters, aged sixty-two, waving her arms angrily, as if shooing away the audience. She wears a shabby but clean dressing-gown, with formal court shoes and stockings. She protects her new hairdo with a fine net and wears spectacles throughout the scene

Peace Get away before I poison the lot of you! Filthy vermin! Blast and curse you when I've just cleaned the window sill. BRIDIE! The pigeons have done their business again.

Bridie, aged sixty-six, bustles on with the gilded tea trolley. She is similarly dressed to Peace but wears a better-looking dressing-gown underneath the shabby one

Bridie Leave that window shut before the whole flat freezes.
Peace What harm if a bit of fresh air gets in? The heat in this room would have a person suffocated.
Bridie She'll feel the cold here after coming from Australia. Sure it's so hot out there, they're used to walking around in their bare feet.
Peace Why doesn't she come in summer so? What's going on that she has to come to London now, and it nearly Christmas. And without the husband. And why does she have to arrive at this hour?
Bridie Now Peace, don't start all that. She can't help what time the plane gets in.
Peace She's her father's daughter and always has been. Selfish to the core.
Bridie (*sing-song*) That's enough, Peace.
Peace I'm the one who had to move all my stuff so Her Royal Highness can have the room. I'm the one who'll be sleeping in that—that *icebox* at the end of the passage. I'll say what I like and I'll say it to her face too, if I feel like it. It's my room as much as it's hers.
Bridie Don't agitate me, Peace. Cheer yourself up now and get changed. Look at the cut of us and Brenda about to walk in.

Peace exits

(*To the audience*) She resents it when my daughter comes home, for fear she won't be Queen of the Heap around here. I don't know why I put up with her. I'd him in there (*she indicates Desmond*) bossing me around for donkey's years and now she's taken over. And talk about touchy! The least little thing sets her off. Just like a child.

Peace enters with the chair

Peace When you've finished talking to yourself, your daughter's on the doorstep.
Bridie (*flustered*) Lord save us! (*She pulls off her dressing-gown, revealing a better one underneath. She hastily rolls up the old one and tosses it to Peace*)

Peace exits

Brenda, aged about forty, enters. She is wearing a jacket, skirt and blouse under a fur coat

Brenda (*warmly*) Hi Mum.

Bridie goes to Brenda and leads her to CS. *They are a little ill-at-ease with each another, but trying hard. They kiss and hug*

Bridie Straight into the front room—into the warm. Well. Are you dead? Not a wink of sleep on the plane, I suppose.
Brenda I slept like a log and I feel terrific
Bridie Kettle's on. Aren't we great to be up so early? You nearly caught the two of us in our old dressing-gowns.

Peace enters. She is also wearing a better gown

Brenda (*moving towards Peace*) Hello Aunty Peace!
Peace (*recoiling*) Don't touch me unless you want chilblains. My hands are like ice from being in that end bedroom.

Peace presents her cheek, Brenda kisses it

Is the kettle on, Bridie?
Bridie You know well it is.

Bridie helps Brenda out of her fur coat. She feels its heft

Oh the weight of this would have you worn out. The fake ones are nice and light. All the rich and famous wear fake ones these days.
Brenda Actually, it's—
Peace The hooligans are pretending to be interested in animal conservation now. A woman on the underground had her fur coat shaved bald and nobody lifted a hand to help her.
Brenda It's fake. A fun fur. Not the real thing. OK?
Bridie (*after a pause*) Well if it looks that real, you might as well wear the real thing instead of going round in a fake. Anyway. Let's look at you: I must say you don't seem a day older.

Brenda Neither do you or Peace. You look really well.

Bridie Oh, now ...

Bridie exits bashfully

Peace moves to the sofa and sits

Peace Well, I'm glad you think so, because neither of us is at all well. Your mother is in constant discomfort from rheumatism and I've terrible pains in my gums since this cold weather started. We never get out—except to Mass, or when there's nothing in the house to eat. We're like prisoners here, day after day. We might as well be dead. That's how well we are.

Brenda You'll feel better in summer, I'm sure you will. But I wish you hadn't changed rooms, I don't mind where I sleep.

Peace I told your mother that, but she wouldn't listen to me. Anyway, it's done now and as long as it's only temporary ...

Bridie enters with the milk jug, and puts it on the trolley

Brenda (*uneasily*) Of course it's only temporary ... New curtains, Mum? They're lovely.

Bridie Thanks, love.

Bridie exits

Peace I was just thinking to myself that if you weren't going to notice them we'd wasted our time making them. I thought you'd say something the minute you came in.

Brenda (*reasonably*) Give us a chance. I mean they don't exactly jump out at a person. They're exactly the same colour as the old ones ... (*uncertainly*) aren't they?

Bridie enters carrying the sugar bowl

Bridie These are mushroom. The old ones were beige. We might as well have kept them if you can't see the difference. Well, I must say Brenda, I thought you were more observant. Not a word about the new trolley. I bet you think it's common.

Bridie exits huffily

Peace (*calling after her*) It *is* common. Sure every Tom, Dick and Harry round here has a tea trolley. She didn't mention it because she doesn't like it. Last time she was here she didn't even notice the new bedspread.

Brenda Yes, I did. I distinctly remember admiring it. And I *do* like the new trolley and the ... the ... (*She looks around, then triumphantly seizes on the sofa*) the new upholstery!

Bridie enters with the last of the tea things. She puts them down rather firmly

Bridie The upholstery hasn't been changed.

Peace She knows it hasn't. She's just being a smart-alec. I told you now Bridie, not to be spending money to impress people, when it's just the two of us.

Brenda (*trying to keep things light*) Visitors might drop in ...
Peace What visitors? You're not at home now dear, you're at *home*.

Bridie hands out the cups of tea, first to Peace, then to Brenda

Bridie Here we are now. Sugar's in.
Brenda Sorry to be a pest Mum, but I don't take milk or sugar in mine.
Bridie Oh? Since when?
Brenda About fifteen years.
Bridie Well, that's strange. Because it's the first I've heard of it.
Peace Throw it down the drain so if she doesn't want it.
Bridie Black tea. Out of the blue. You remind me of your father, pretending
    to like his meat underdone.

*The Lights come up on Desmond. He becomes alert and reacts now that he's
being discussed*

Brenda (*smiling*) Maybe he really *did* like his meat underdone.

Desmond reacts

Bridie Indeed he did not. That was all put on, trying to impress people.

Desmond reacts

Peace It's probably smart, in Australia, but can you imagine what black tea
    does to the lining of your stomach?
Bridie The tannin, you mean? Sure tannin's more poisonous than nicotine.
Brenda (*showing strain*) I'll *drink* it, OK? No problem at all. (*She drains her
    cup and slams cup and saucer down on the trolley*)
Bridie (*wounded*) There was no need for that, Brenda. No need at all. How
    were we supposed to know you suddenly stopped taking milk and sugar?
    We'll know for the next time.
Brenda That's OK then.
Peace Does "he" take milk in his?
Brenda No, "he" doesn't.
Bridie ⎱
Peace ⎰ (*together, triumphantly*) Aha.
Peace Bridie and I had a great idea, to simplify our tea drinking. I used to
    take *two* sugars and Bridie used to take *one*. So we split the difference and
    now we both take one and a half and it doesn't matter if the cups get
    mixed up.

Peace and Bridie swap cups, drink and shrug

    Aren't we sensible?
Brenda (*smiling*) Very sensible.
Peace (*chidingly but with affection*) I don't suppose *you* had the sense to
    bring a warm dressing-gown?
Brenda Not very warm, no. I don't seem to need one at home.
Bridie Peace and I have wardrobes full. All warm ones. Quilted. Mohair.
    Double Flannel. Pure wool with lining. Zipper, button, sash. Mostly
    Harrods sales, though Marks have new ones in.

Peace (*scornfully*) Sure they look like duvets. Big humpy backs on them.

Bridie I said to your Aunty Peace: Peace, I said, we're always in our gowns, so let's have a selection for fear we'd get sick of the sight of ourselves.

Brenda (*smiling*) Dad wouldn't approve. Remember how he hated to see us in our gowns?

Desmond reacts

Bridie (*ignoring her*) Remember your cousins in Cork and they always in their coats? Sure nothing looks worse than a coat worn over night attire.

Peace Does His Nibs wear a gown?

Brenda (*carefully*) 'Course he does. A nice towelling one with his initials monogrammed on the pocket.

Peace (*after a pause*) Do you not think that's a bit nancy-boy? We'd say that was nancy-boy, wouldn't we, Bridie?

Bridie I must say, a monogram doesn't seem manly somehow. Could you unpick it?

Brenda (*snapping*) I don't want to unpick it!

Desmond is delighted

Bridie Well, we only asked. I don't know where you get that touchiness. There was never any touchiness in our family.

Peace I suppose I'll get my head bitten off if I ask how long you're staying?

Brenda (*making a big effort to relax*) Ah, well that depends on Bonny, my agent. I'll be seeing her later this morning.

Bridie (*wounded*) On your first day home, is it?

Peace Sure this is just a depot for her. A place to drop off her luggage.

Brenda I'm sorry. But she's terribly busy and she said today. We have so much to discuss. I sent her the final draft of a new play about a month ago. She's a marvellous agent—there's a good chance she's sold it.

Bridie Did you hear about a one called Victoria Wood out there? She won an award. I'd say she's a bit younger than you, Bren. Would you, Peace?

Peace Oh indeed she is—and she's very good.

Brenda (*firmly*) I'm very good too.

Bridie But there's no comparison. She makes everything up. You're inclined to put members of your family into your plays. Victoria Wood makes everything up.

Brenda What makes you think she doesn't use members of *her* family?

Bridie I just know she wouldn't. She seems a nice sort of girl. Family-minded. Anyone could tell that poor creature in your last effort was your Uncle Pat.

Peace (*deadly*) Our *brother*!

Brenda (*digging in her briefcase for press clippings*) Look: All the best writing reflects real life. Ask Victoria Wood if you think she's such an expert.

Bridie I don't need to ask anybody. I just wish you'd write something nice that we could enjoy without feeling embarrassed. Nobody else in the family went.

Brenda Did you tell them it was on?

Bridie ⎫ (*together*) We certainly did not!
Peace ⎭
Brenda Thanks a lot.

Desmond perks up, hoping for a fight

Bridie It would be different if you wrote something with a proper story to it. A comedy. Victoria Wood writes funny stuff and she won an award. People don't want to be depressed.
Brenda (*handing over two batches of clippings and standing behind the sofa*) Hold everything till you've read these: The reviews of my latest. A comedy!
Bridie Let's have a look.

Peace and Bridie put on specs—Peace adding a second pair. They seem engrossed in Brenda's reviews

Bridie (*to Brenda*) Oh! I didn't tell you the news. Over the road's daughter went to live in New Zealand and sent back photos of the house if you please. A big blue swimming pool and acres of lawn. Can you imagine, and she a shop assistant when she lived here. Tsk.
Peace (*reading*) How do *we* know it's her house? Maybe she was just posing in front of it.
Brenda (*to Peace*) Not bad, eh?
Peace (*to Brenda*) Are the papers out there up to date? Did you see where the footballers were killed in France? The President went to the funeral for all the good it did anybody.
Bridie (*reflecting*) Well. They'd expect him to go. (*She pauses*) He couldn't very well *not* go. When I think of those young lads, I could just weep.
Brenda (*pointing to a cutting in Peace's hand*) That's me, at the opening . . .

Peace and Bridie remove their glasses and rub their eyes

Bridie Our eyes get tired. Too much television, I suppose.
Peace It's old age.
Bridie No, it's the telly. They say it's bad to watch too much. The flickering of the picture can bring on fits. Especially if you're a dormant epileptic. A doctor on the radio said that.
Brenda (*angrily taking back her clippings*) Not remotely interested, are you? If they were Victoria bloody Wood's reviews you'd have them framed.

Desmond perks up

Peace That's a nice way to speak to your mother!
Brenda (*putting the clippings back in her briefcase*) You mind your own business.
Bridie Leave Peace out of this. You're like a child, expecting praise every two minutes. How can we get excited about a play we haven't seen?
Brenda (*angrily*) Because it was written by *me*. By your daughter!
Peace (*jumping up excitedly*) That's it. Screech away. Screech away. (*She suddenly freezes in a bent position*) Jesus Mary and Joseph, Bridie, my back's gone . . . my back . . . my back.

Desmond rocks with delight

Bridie (*helping Peace to the arm of the sofa*) Keep calm now Peace till we see. (*She prepares to manipulate Peace's back*)

Peace Careful, Bridie. You were very rough the last time.

Brenda Does this happen regularly? Or only when I come home . . . ?

Bridie As you well know, your aunt's back goes out when she gets emotional. Are you ready, Peace?

Peace ⎫   I wandered lonely as a cloud that floats on high o'er vales
    ⎬ (*together*)   and hills . . .
Bridie ⎭   One, two, three and—(*She gives Peace's shoulders a good wrench*)

Peace's posture returns to normal

Peace (*meekly*) Thanks very much, Bridie.

Brenda Fully recovered?

Peace (*sitting weakly on the sofa*) No thanks to you and your bawling and the neighbours all ears. I think I'll have to wear my collar for a while Bridie. I've a weak feeling between my vertebrae.

Brenda paces about

Bridie Wear it so. Will you stop fidgeting Brenda, you're making us nervous.

Brenda (*making a supreme effort*) Look, I'm probably a bit jet-lagged and I've a lot on my mind at the moment—what with going to see Bonny and everything. I'm sorry, Mum.

Desmond reacts scornfully; he is bored by attempts at peace-keeping

Bridie (*magnanimously*) No apologies necessary. Sure flying makes your whole system go haywire. Relax there for a few minutes. Can I get you anything? (*She eases Brenda into the chair*) More tea?

Brenda (*relieved*) No thanks, Mum. Tell you what, though. I'd love an English newspaper. Do you still get it delivered?

Peace (*after a pause*) It's in your father's room. He has to have first read of it.

Brenda (*smiling*) What?

Bridie Do you want the paper, love?

Peace Ask your mother if you don't believe me. The paper goes in there for an hour every morning, come hail, rain or shine . . .

Bridie What harm if it does? It's my paper. I'll leave it on the roof if I want to.

Peace If you think that's normal behaviour, look at the face on Brenda. I have to sleep in a room the size of a coal cellar while his ghost is in there reading the morning paper in luxury.

Bridie I'll go and get it for you, Brenda.

Brenda No, I'll go.

Brenda, watched by Peace and Bridie, walks to Desmond's area. If there's a door it should be open. Brenda stops on the threshold

We hear the theme music, faint and disorted. The lights dim

Desmond (*not looking at her*) I'd be a liar if I said I missed you. I didn't, and that's all about it.

Brenda walks slowly into the room and picks up the newspaper from the bed. She returns to the others and sits down. The Lights come up

Peace Read it so, once you've got it.

Bridie Let her be. She'll read it when she feels like it.

Peace (*louder and louder*) She does everything when she feels like it. Ask her why she's home in the middle of winter. Ask her if she'll be waking up the whole block with her toilet flushing and bathing at all hours, like she did the last time. Not a drop of hot water left for anybody else. No consideration for—

Brenda (*covering her ears*) Leave me alone!

Bridie (*whispering*) Keep it down! Do you want him to have the satisfaction of hearing us fighting and you hardly in the door?

Brenda (*shouting*) For God's sake Mum, he's been dead five years. We can shout as much as we like. He's dead. And who cares!

Desmond reacts with indignation

Bridie That's lovely talk from a daughter about her father, God rest his soul.

Desmond agrees

Brenda You have a short memory when it suits you. (*She mocks an often heard complaint of her mother's*) And who was the man who stopped going to Mass the minute he had the ring on your finger?

Bridie That sarcasm has never suited you, Brenda. He had his faults like everybody else, and why wouldn't he and he a sick man for the best part of his life? He did his best when all's said and done. And I'll tell you something that'll annoy you: There's a lot about you that reminds us of him! Isn't *that* a wonder!

Peace and Desmond concur

Brenda That's nonsense! Anyway, I'd better get cracking if I want to miss the rush hour. I'll be back about six, OK?

She grabs for her coat. Flustered, she puts her arm into the wrong sleeve and has to begin again. She picks up her briefcase

Brenda exits

The Light on Desmond fades. He exits, pushing his bed

Peace There's something going on there. The strained face of her—and hardly a mention of "him".

Bridie It's nothing to do with you. She's my daughter. (*She begins to push off the sofa*)

Peace gathers the tea things and puts them on the trolley

Peace You're welcome to her. (*She picks up the newspaper and hands it to Bridie*) Here. The head of the house didn't get his full hour. I'm going back to bed. I still don't see why she couldn't have arrived at a more convenient time. (*She begins pushing the trolley off*) But that one has always been full of her own importance—ever since the day she was born.

Peace exits with the trolley

We hear 40s music and the static of a radio being tuned

The actors for Scene 2 enter, bringing their props

SCENE 2

1941. The Pub Scene. A small Dublin bar

A Barman finishes the tuning of a radio on the bar counter. We hear pips as he locates the news station

Brenda enters, dressed as in Scene 1. She slips off her fur coat, hangs it in the wing. She sits on the stool, an observer

A 40s style newscast is heard on the pub radio

Announcer This is the BBC Home Service. Here is the news. The United States Navy suffered severe losses this morning when Japanese aircraft bombed Pearl Harbor in Hawaii. President Roosevelt, speaking in a nation-wide broadcast, said ninety-four naval——
Barman (*switching off the radio*) Same ould news every night.

Desmond, aged thirty, enters, walking angily. He wears a raincoat

Are you a father yet, Desmond?
Desmond A bloody girl! Wouldn't you think she did it to spite me? Jaysus, you'd swear she did.
Barman Ah, don't be blowing up like an ould vulcano. Didn't many a great fella have nothing but daughters?
Desmond *What* great fella had nothing but daughters?
Barman (*after a pause*) Many a fella, many a fella. Whiskey is it, Desmond?
Desmond You know well it is. And here's Mooney—with the big artificial grin on him.

Mooney enters. Seeing Desmond, he freezes comically, cupping a hand to his ear

Mooney Do I hear a boy?
Barman You don't—and your man has a sour puss on him over it.
Mooney (*approaching the bar*) Twas a girl then?
Desmond Well what other bloody choice is there! Aren't you a great detective Mooney?
Mooney (*cheerfully*) Well, maybe I'm not, but the drinks are on me, lads— compliments of the German Reparation Fund. (*He looks gratefully*

towards the sky). Wasn't it the lucky ould bomb they dropped near Dublin, the ejits, and they flying over the wrong country entirely, God Bless them! (*He produces a wad of notes*)

The Barman pours three generous shots of whiskey, and leaves the bottle on the bar. Desmond drinks morosely

Barman Have you not that spent, and a week gone by? You must have put in a good-size claim then, Mooney?

Mooney Arra, I could have stretched it a bit more than I did, I suppose, but I didn't want to overdo it like some of them. Did you hear about the McBrides? Claimed for six pigs and they thirty miles from where the bomb dropped. At least my cow was in the bloody vicinity.

Barman So was it just the one cow you claimed?

Mooney Indeed it wasn't. Didn't I put in for a stud bull or two while I was at it. But the McBrides laid it on a bit thick. They say her nibs claimed for a new carpet.

Barman Go 'way.

Mooney Said the heat of the blast flattened the pile of the one she had. Sure the likes of them spoil it for everybody. The Gerry will be more watchful now. They say everyone within a radius of fifty miles demanded reparation for broken windows.

Desmond A bloody girl. Sure nobody really wants daughters, there's no point to them, except for helping their mother round the house.

Mooney Come on now, Des. I bet she's a grand little thing, and your Missus such a lovely looking woman.

Desmond Indeed she's not.

Mooney (*indignantly*) Bridie not lovely, is it! I'm telling you Desmond, you were lucky to marry a one the likes of Bridie, and she so ladylike.

Desmond I'm talking about the child, Mooney. She's as ugly as sin with the big red face and the spikey hair. I'll tell you straight, it's not a baby I could take to.

Brenda smiles

Barman They say Flannigan claimed the bomb killed his mother and she dead a week.

Mooney (*amused*) That's a good one. (*Pause*) Did he get anything?

Barman Still arguing the case. He got a letter from the Germans saying they couldn't be held responsible for people dying *before* the bomb dropped. So Flannigan wrote back and said 'twas the premonition that killed her.

Mooney (*laughing delightedly*) Isn't that a good one, Des? That's the best yet! Cheer up now and we'll toast the young one. You've plenty of time to have sons and you a fine healthy young fella.

Desmond I can't help it I tell you. I didn't want a girl and that's all about it. Sure I'm not cut out to be a family man, that's the tragedy of it.

Mooney We'll toast it ourselves so, myself and himself. Has the child a name?

Desmond (*with great reluctance*) Brenda.

Mooney Right. To Brenda Barnes.

Barman ⎱ (*together*) God bless her
Mooney ⎰

The Barman and Mooney raise their glasses

Desmond exits, ignoring the toast

Brenda slips off her shoes and jacket and puts on short white socks and school sandals

As the bar set is struck we hear Glenn Miller or other forties dance music

SCENE 3

1950. The Courtroom Scene. The bedroom of the Barnes' house in Dublin. Late at night

Desmond, aged forty, enters tugging Brenda, aged nine, along behind him. He directs her to a stool and she climbs onto it, her legs dangling childishly

Desmond gets onto the bed, uses a whiskey bottle to rap three times on his bedside table. He is nicely propped up, looks very comfortable

Desmond Right. The court is now in session. From here on, the accused will address the judge as "Your Lordship". State your name, age and place of residence.

Brenda Brenda Barnes, aged nine. Twenty one St Dominic's Road, Sandymount, Dublin, Ireland, Eur—

Desmond And do you swear to tell the truth, the whole truth and nothing but the truth?

Brenda I do, Your Lordship.

Desmond Now: The plaintiff has told the court that on the evening of March the sixth he purchased a box of Black Magic chocolates. On retiring to bed the same evening, opened the box and selected and ate a Strawberry Cup, guided by the illustration so thoughtfully provided by the manufacturer. Exhibit One. (*He holds up the flavour guide*) Are ye all familiar with Exhibit One?

Brenda Yes, Daddy.

Desmond What's that you said?

Brenda Yes, your Lordship.

Desmond Good. Then I'll proceed. The plaintiff, before retiring on the evening of the following day, March the seventh, opened the box and again consulted the flavour guide. In the mood for a crunchy centre, he decided on a Chocolate Nut Cluster and reached into the box, thus: (*He mimes reaching in, looks askance, withdraws his hand, demonstrates that the space is empty*) And what do you think he found?

Brenda (*tentatively*) Nothing, your Lordship?

Desmond Nuthin. In the little brown nest meant to contain the Chocolate Nut Cluster, the plaintiff found thin air. An empty space. So where does that leave the plaintiff?

Brenda Don't know, your Lordship.

Desmond I put it to you that The Plaintiff was extremely disappointed. And that he immediately thought of a suspect by the name of Brenda Barnes. Now a person might be inclined to say that the removal of a Chocolate Nut Cluster is, in itself, a not very serious crime. But, when the suspect has been pacif—suspif—*specifically* told to stay clear of The Plaintiff's private box of chocolates, the matter must be viewed in a different light, and seen as the mean, sneaky crime that it actually is.

Brenda swings her legs absent-mindedly, infuriating Desmond

(*With real venom*) I've always seen through you—you little gobshite!

Brenda stops swinging her legs

(*Shouting*) Sit up and pay attention! Confess that you ate it while I'm still in a good humour.

Bridie, aged thirty-eight, in a dressing-gown, bursts in, very agitated

Brenda climbs off the stool

(*To Brenda*) Back in the dock. Prisoner back in the dock.

Brenda sits down again

Bridie How long more are you going to keep this up? She'll never get up for school at this rate? I ask you, a grown man playing "courtrooms" to amuse himself. You ought to be ashamed.

Desmond (*mockingly*) Here she is, in her dressing-gown. Competition for Maureen O'Sullivan.

Bridie She's asleep on her feet, the poor child. For pity's sake let me tuck her in. Can't you have a whatchamacallit: an adjournment?

Desmond Not till the prisoner confesses.

Bridie exits, muttering

Desmond You took it, didn't you Brenda?

Brenda No, Daddy.

Desmond Own up now and we'll all get some sleep.

Brenda I can't, Daddy. Sure I can't own up if I didn't take it.

Desmond Would you be willing to have fingerprints taken?

Brenda (*faintly*) Fingerprints?

Desmond Yes. Fingerprints that'll prove 'twas you. We'll go down to the police station first thing in the morning and have them done. Unless you'd like to own up now . . .

Brenda (*scared stiff*) I can't Daddy. Sure I didn't take it.

Desmond (*incoherent*) Very well. The prosecution rests . . ., the court will take a short recess . . .

His voice tails off and he falls into a deep, snore-laden sleep, the cigarette alight in his hand. After a couple of snores, Brenda very cautiously withdraws the missing chocolate from the pocket of her skirt. She dusts it off, tiptoes to the box and puts the chocolate into it. She freezes as Desmond stirs, then tiptoes back to the stool

We become aware of the ticking of a clock. Brenda falls asleep, her upturned face falling to one side

Smoke begins to issue from Desmond's bedclothes. He and Brenda sleep on

   Bridie enters and rushes to Desmond's bed

Brenda jumps off the stool

Bridie Sweet Holy Mary! Wake up, Desmond! Wake up, wake up!

Desmond leaps out of bed with amazing alacrity. Bridie thumps out the fire and bundles up the bedding, the bundle revealing a smouldered sheet

   (*While thumping*) How many times have I warned you about smoking in bed!

Desmond That does it. The brat tried to murder me.

Bridie Why didn't you call me, Brenda? Can you imagine what the neighbours would say if they heard you let your Daddy smoulder. You bad girl.

Desmond The ungrateful brat. Wasn't I right not to like her?

Bridie (*to Brenda*) And what about me? If I caught fire it wouldn't matter, I suppose?

Desmond Enough's enough. You can send her to your mother's in Galway for a few months.

Brenda (*distressed, to Bridie*) I don't want to go to Galway. I want to go to England! You said we were going to England!

Bridie Sure we *are* going to England. And when we're settled we'll send for you. Won't we Daddy?

Desmond (*to Bridie*) *I'm* going to England, on my own, till I get things organized. And she's going to Galway first thing tomorrow morning. First thing.

Brenda and Bridie look at him aghast

   All right, I'm not an unreasonable man. (*He pauses*) She can go in the evening. (*He affects a pitiful voice*) Will you see to it for me, Bridie?

Bridie (*placatingly*) Indeed I will, Desmond, indeed I will. Come downstairs now pet, till I make you hot milk.

Bridie and Desmond exit, Bridie carrying the burnt bundle

Desmond (*whining, as he exits*) I'm lucky to be alive, sweetheart. That child's always had it in for me, and I doing my best to be a family man.

Bridie (*as she goes*) All right love, all right.

Brenda stomps over to the chocolate box, retrieves the chocolate and pops it into her mouth. She crunches it noisily and defiantly but after a while her face crumples and she begins to cry silently. She childishly wipes her eyes with her fist

We hear the sound of a steam train's whistle

Brenda sits on the stool and begins to sway, as if on board a train

We hear the train pulling out of the station and gathering speed

The train is dark and Brenda's bleak face is lit intermittently by the lights of a train passing in the other direction

Brenda climbs off the stool, puts it on the bed, and pushes the bed off

The train sound effect gives way to a schoolgirls' choir

SCENE 4

1950. The Convent Scene. The office of Mother Superior, a Dominican nun

There is a large statue of the Virgin Mary and a low stool. Mother Superior is pacing up and down. A timid knock is heard

Mother Superior Enter.

Brenda, aged nine, enters and halts. She is wearing a school blazer

Come in properly, Brenda Barnes. You may sit.

Brenda curtseys and sits on the stool, facing downstage

Brenda Thank you, Mother.
Mother Superior Do you know why I wanted to see you, Brenda Barnes?
Brenda No, Mother.
Mother Superior Sister Francesca tells me you've been thinking dirty thoughts and making remarks that would offend the Sweet Virgin Mary, Mother of Baby Jesus our Saviour.
Brenda (*softly*) Yes, Mother.
Mother Superior You're a strange child, Brenda Barnes, with an unfortunate history. But I agreed to let you attend this school to please your Grandmother. Now: did you never ask your mother where you came from?
Brenda I did, Mother.
Mother Superior And what did she tell you?
Brenda She said I came from St Margaret's Nursing Home in Sandymount, Mother.

Mother Superior sighs deeply. She produces a large hinged biscuit tin from beneath her tabard

Mother Superior Have you any idea what this biscuit tin contains, Brenda Barnes?
Brenda No, Mother.
Mother Superior If I told you this biscuit tin contained the key to the divine mystery of procreation, would you have an understanding of what I'm saying, child?
Brenda No, Mother.

Mother Superior rolls her eyes

Mother Superior Let us pray.

Brenda hastily slides off her stool and kneels, her hands joined neatly. The prayers and responses are very fast

    Repeat after me: Sweet Virgin Mary, Mother of God . . .

Brenda Sweet Virgin Mary, Mother of God . . .

Mother Superior Be with us in our hour of need.

Brenda Be with us in our hour of need.

Mother Superior Cleanse our minds of evil thoughts and let the knowledge we are about to receive enrich our hearts . . .

Brenda Cleanse our minds of evil thoughts and let the knowledge we are about to receive enrich our hearts . . .

Mother Superior Amen.

Brenda Amen.

Mother Superior opens the hinged biscuit tin carefully and stands behind Brenda

Mother Superior Open your eyes, sit, and hold the biscuit tin, Brenda Barnes.

Brenda sits on the stool and Mother Superior puts the biscuit tin into her hands. She holds it chest-high. Mother Superior rolls back her voluminous sleeves, reaches into the tin and withdraws a boudoir biscuit and a doughnut. She holds them at arm's length, crucifixion style. She demonstrates the doughnut first, swinging her arm around slowly until the doughnut is positioned right under the startled Brenda's nose

    The doughnut represents the entrance to the female reproductive system, situated down below and called The Vagina. (*She swings out the doughnut, swings in the boudoir biscuit*) The boudoir biscuit represents the exit of the male reproductive system, also situated down below, and called The Penis. (*She swings out the boudoir biscuit, then brings both items in slowly*) Within the holy state of matrimony, the male and female, wishing to procreate in the name of the Lord, draw together with lust-free love and chaste thoughts in their hearts. (*She slowly inserts the end of the boudoir biscuit into the doughnut*) After a short time the Lord in His wisdom releases the male seed from the tip of the boudoir biscuit and causes it to pass through the doughnut in search of an Egg, or Ovum. (*She wiggles the boudoir a little bit*)

Pause

    They say 'tis a beautiful experience.

Pause

    Nine months later the fruit of the womb emerges from the doughnut, and is baptized as soon as possible. (*She separates the doughnut and boudoir biscuit, drops them into the open tin, and briskly brushes off her fingers*) Is there anything you wish to ask me, Brenda Barnes?

Brenda No, Mother.

Mother Superior So you now have a complete understanding of how Our Lord in his wisdom designed our bodies for procreation within the blessed bounds of matrimony?

Brenda Yes, Mother.

Mother Superior Then I'll be on my way. You will meditate on the wondrous knowledge you have just received. You will not discuss our meeting with any other girl in the school. And you will never touch yourself down below except when bathing, at which time you will avert your eyes and fill your mind with thoughts of the innocent Virgin Mary. Now you may relax there quietly enjoying the refreshments. God Bless you, Brenda Barnes.

Brenda takes the doughnut and biscuit

   Mother Superior exits taking the stool and biscuit tin with her

Brenda studies the biscuit and doughnut for a while, then cautiously inserts the biscuit into the doughnut. Deeply puzzled, she looks in the direction of Mother Superior's exit, then absent-mindedly raises the boudoir biscuit to her mouth and takes a bite out of it

The scene change music is heard

   Brenda skips cheerfully off

   Bella and Peace bring on a bed and wardrobe

   Brenda, aged eleven, enters immediately with her notebook and pencil

SCENE 5

1951. The Bella Scene. A bedroom in Granny Cleary's house in Galway

Brenda, aged eleven, and Peace, aged thirty-three, are sitting on a bed. Brenda is writing in her notebook. Peace, wearing a dressing-gown, is knitting. Both of them keep an eye on Bella Rafferty, a neighbour of theirs who has dropped in to use the mirror of their wardrobe

Bella Thanks for the use of the mirror, girls. Living in Galway really cramps a person's style. The ructions next door if I put a bit of lipstick on—and I nearly eighteen!

Peace I wouldn't bother myself with fellas. Just wouldn't bother myself. All sweet talk in the beginning, then making a skivvy of you later on.

Bella Ah, don't mind your Aunty Peace, Brenda. You know something girls? I love my legs. Love, *love*, LOVE them! (*She inspects her legs, mouths a kiss at them*) See the way they go in and out where they're supposed to? Well-shaped legs must touch at the tops of the thighs, the knees, the calves and the ankles. (*She reveals her legs and demonstrates*)

Peace (*fighting for Brenda's attention*) ... and men aren't a bit hygienic. You'll never see a man bothering to wash his hands when he's been to visit the toilet. No, I'm not bothering. Thank God I had brothers so I found out what men are like. Big *goms* expecting to be waited on hand and foot. No thanks.

Bella A well-placed waist should be opposite the bend in your elbow.

Bella demonstrates. Brenda examines her own waistline

Peace Whenever I hear a person's having a baby I even say a prayer it'll be a girl. So don't be bothering with talk about boys, now, Brenda. Study to be a typist and you'll have a great life so you will (*She puts down her knitting for a moment*). Imagine a job where you sit down all day. 'Twould be heavenly.

Brenda I'm going to England to be a writer. You can do anything in England and they don't laugh at you.

Peace That's what you think. Anyway, writing isn't for the likes of us. Study to be a typist or you'll end up a shop assistant like me and her.

Bella If you listen to your Aunty Peace you'll have the life of an ould nun, Brenda. If I say so myself, haven't I lovely little white hands? (*She inspects Brenda's hands*) Let's see yours: No, loveen, they'll be big. I can tell by your knuckles. I expect your mother has big hands. I've always found that men prefer small ones.

Peace Who asked you to waltz in here giving out opinions? My sister Bridie was always gorgeous, and she had loads of fellas after her. And a better class than the ones sniffing around you, Bella Rafferty!

Bella Why did she marry such a yoke, so? Not bad in the looks department, but I hear he's a fella that does nothing but snooze between jars. Nothing personal Brenda, but they say your Dad's run off to London and your Mam's gone searching for him, and you dumped here while they're off gallivanting!

Brenda My Daddy went ahead to get everything arranged and they'll send for me when my bedroom is ready. I'm having wallpaper covered with ballerinas.

Peace Ballerinas! I wish you'd get your head out of the clouds, Brenda, and you a big girl of eleven.

Bella Isn't my hair lovely and shiny? I broke an egg into the last rinse. They say you've your father's hair, Brenda. The thickness of it! (*To Peace*) Like what you'd find growing over a horse's arse!

Peace jumps up, pulling at Brenda

Peace You're disgusting, talking like that in front of the child. (*To Brenda*) Come downstairs with me till she's gone, the way you won't hear any more smut.

Bella Stay with me, Brenda, and learn about the interesting side of life.

Brenda is torn, then opts for Bella's company

Brenda I'll be down in a minute, Aunty Peace . . .

Peace gives Brenda a sharp smack on the shoulder

Peace Please yourself!

Peace exits

Bella God, your Aunty Peace is awful crabby, Brenda. But I suppose she never really recovered from that bullseye business.

Brenda What bullseye business?

Bella Do you mean to tell me you don't know what caused your Aunty Peace's bad nerves and poor eyesight? Well, you must be the only person in Galway that *doesn't* know. Two boys from St Luke's Reformatory followed her to the tidal pool one day. "Tell me," says one of them, "are you fond of bull's eyes?" "Course I am" says your Aunty Peace, "bullseyes are my favourites." "Well we put a couple in your blazer pockets for you," says the other lad, "we thought you'd be hungry after your swim." "Thanks very much", says your Aunty Peace. And didn't she put her hands into her blazer pockets and didn't she draw out two big bull's eyes, a right and a left, fresh from the butchers, with bits of veins and *schkin* and eyelashes still attached to them.

Brenda I think I'm going to faint.

Bella That's exactly what your Aunty Peace said. And she did. And when she came to she needed glasses, and no amount of Novenas made any difference.

Brenda reaches for her notebook

Brenda The poor thing. Will I put that in a story, or would people say it was an exaggeration?

Bella You and your stories!

Bella jumps onto the bed and arranges herself to advantage. She grabs Brenda by the front of her blouse

C'mere young one. C'mere till I tell you a secret—and I'll break your face if you say a word about it. I was in Café Daphne's yesterday and didn't this fella with a moustache invite me over to his table! "Have a cup of tea and a few cakes", says he, pushing the plate over. I accepted the tea but I wouldn't give him the satisfaction of having a cake. A cup of tea is nothing, but a fella like that might think I'd be gawping over a few ould cakes. Anyway: "You've lovely eyes," says he, "are you a visitor from Dublin?". I told him I wasn't, sipping the tea as if I couldn't be bothered. "You're never a local girl," says he, "you've the air of a big place like Dublin on you". "And what air is on you?" says I . . .

Brenda *(enthralled)* And he said?

Bella He said he was on holidays—*from the Seminary*! And I said he better not be admiring my eyes so, and he a priest.

Brenda Janey Mack!

Bella "I'm not a priest *yet*" says he, "will you go for a walk?" "Oh," says I, "I thought you'd be in a car with all the smart talk". "I've a car parked outside," says he. "I'm not sure I could be bothered," says I, and asked him had it a hood on it.

Brenda And had it?

Bella It had. A big black thing—the likes of what you'd see on a baby's pram. Next thing the two of us are on a spin out the coast road. "Tell me now," says I, "when you've your dog collar on, does it stick in your Adam's apple?" He said it did and asked me would I kiss the place better.

Brenda (*astonished*) And did you?

Bella I did—and he kissed the beauty spot behind my ear, so I told him to stop the car quick for fear of an accident! The compliments he had for me! He said they'd told him at the Seminary he must expose himself to the world outside before making his final decision—that's why he was on holidays, testing himself to see could he resist temptation.

Brenda And could he?

There is a long, loaded pause during which Bella's smug expression implies that the answer will be "he couldn't"

Bella He could.

Brenda (*fervently*) Oh, isn't that great? His Guardian Angel must've been watching over him.

Bella (*giving a cheeky laugh*) His Guardian Angel will be wore out so, because his nibs and I have another date this evening. That's where I'm going now and I twenty minutes late on purpose!

Brenda (*a bit thrilled*) I . . . I think what you're doing is a sin, Bella Rafferty.

Bella (*ignoring her*) . . . And when it's all over I'm going to open my big eyes and look at him and say, "Could you ever bless me, Father?" Can you imagine the face he'll have on him? I'll tell you something: I could get anyone to love me! *Anyone*—even the Pope! (*She laughs and poses, in love with herself*)

Granny's steps are heard approaching

Brenda My granny's coming up the stairs!

Bella abruptly stops laughing and buttons up her neckline more modestly

Granny enters, huffing and puffing

Granny Have you finished your homework, Brenda?

Brenda I have.

Granny (*to Bella*) And what are you doing out at this hour?

Bella (*pulling on a headscarf*) I'm going down to the church, Mrs Cleary, to make a Novena.

Brenda conceals a giggle. Unseen by Granny, Bella waves a threatening fist in Brenda's face. Granny opens the wardrobe door, revealing a large holy picture on the back of it, complete with small red nightlight

Granny Brenda and I are going to bed. We may as well. 'Tis warmer up here than down below. Let yourself out quietly, there's a good girl.

Bella I will, Mrs Cleary. Bye bye Brenda. I'll be sure to light a candle for you.

She gives Brenda a last violent warning to hush as she exits

Granny (*lighting the nightlight*) Is your mind filled with purity, Brenda love?

Brenda (*looking after Bella*) It is, Granny.

Granny We'll have a good night's sleep, please God. I've a very tiring day tomorrow. I promised Father O'Donnel I'd go down and polish the side

altar candlesticks before eight o'clock mass: I've a meeting of The legion
of Mary at eleven and two Sisters of Mercy will be round for a cup of tea
and a sweet bun at three sharp. Lord give me strength.

*Brenda gets into bed. She watches as Granny undresses. The old woman is lit
by a special as she places a large white tent-like nightdress over her head. It
conceals her from the neck down as she undresses. She wears a surreal number
of garments, which are wrested from the neck and hem of the nightie. She never
removes her grey stockings. The garments worn include the following: a pair of
felt slippers, a black skirt, a black cardigan, a blouse, a grubby pink corset,
hung with suspenders, a long sleeved vest, a short-sleeved vest, a pair of beige
cotton knickers. A gigantic pair of pink bloomers, with elasticated legs*

*As each garment is removed it is placed neatly in the wardrobe. Throughout
the undressing, Granny prays rapidly and Brenda responds, even more rapidly,
her hands joined neatly*

*Granny begins by fetching her night knickers from under the pillow and placing
them neatly on the floor in front of her, the faster to put them on when the time
comes*

Granny (*urgently*) Hail Mary full of grace the Lord is with thee. Blessed art
   Thou among women and blessed is the fruit of Thy womb, Jesus.
Brenda Holy Mary Mother of God pray for us sinners now and at the hour
   of our death Amen.

*The prayer is repeated as often as required, but between the removal of her day
knickers and the putting on of her night knickers, Granny's prayer halts in
midstream. When her night knickers are safely on, Granny resumes the prayer
with renewed fervour*

*Next, Granny turns upstage and appears to remove her teeth, which she
ostentatiously places in a glass, after polishing them on the sleeve of her
nightie. Granny's prayers thereafter have a gummy sound to them. Finally, the
old woman lets down her hair and climbs wearily into bed*

*Brenda stops responding because she has dozed off, so Granny completes the
final prayer herself*

*After a few final mumbles and lipsmacks, Granny falls asleep and delivers a
hearty snore. This cues in the dreamy, rosy lighting and the "Limelight" theme
music. A mirror ball would be effective*

Brenda sits up

   *A young priest enters wearing a white surplice over a red, full-length
   garment, and a white collar. He has a moustache*

*He swaggers, Bogart-style. He takes an old-fashioned cigarette lighter from a
special little pocket sewn in to the surplice and flicks it on, holding the flame
aloft, each small movement choreographed to the music. He lights a cigarette,
blowing the smoke out slowly in Brenda's direction. She rises from the bed. He
stubs out the cigarette and they begin to dance. Their movements are sparse.*

The choreography should be Fred Astaire and Ginger Rogers, and always innocent. Granny snores at strategic moments

During the dance, the priest removes his collar passionately and throws it away

Brenda arabesques as she kisses his adam's apple, then is enraptured as he kisses a spot behind her ear

Finally Brenda returns to the bed. Sitting up, she tempts the priest. He is bashful, then succumbs. He goes to her and she places his hand on her breast. He immediately looks saintly, withdraws his hand

    The priest dances off

Brenda (*clasping her breast with her own hand*) Bless me, Father ... Oh, bless me, Father ...

The lighting reverts to normal and Granny rises up groggily, sees and hears Brenda

Granny (*screeching*) Get your hands off your body this minute! Is it a *Jezebel* we have in the house? Is it? Is it? I'll *brain* you so I will, *brain* you!

Granny chases Brenda around the bed, accompanied by a lively sequence from the theme music

    During the chase, they haul the bed off

If additional dialogue is required

    Fiddling with yourself indeed. What kind of going on is that for a young girl in a decent home.

    Peace enters during the uproar and pushes off the wardrobe

We hear mandolins

SCENE 6

1953. The Café Daphne Scene

The kitchen of a small, scruffy cafe and bed and breakfast establishment, a sign reads "Cafe Daphne's: B & B—Meal's—Mineral's"

Café Daphne bustles on with her "kitchen", all of which can be conveyed on a large trolley. There's a tea urn, baking utensils, big tins etc.

Café Daphne sprinkles coconut on to some tarts

Café Daphne (*consulting her watch*) Jesus, Mary and Joseph is that the time! And not as much as a potato peeled. (*She wipes her nose upwardly with the palm of her hand, then plunges the same hand into the coconut tin*)

    Brenda, aged thirteen, enters, a bit bashfully, carrying a note

Hello, Brenda love.

Brenda Hello, Café Daphne. I've a note from my Aunty Peace.

Café Daphne Leave it down for the moment, love. Sure I'm murdered making coconut tarts and I desperate to visit the butchers. Here y'are now: lick your fingers and have a dip and a suck of that coconut.

Brenda eagerly licks the fingers of her hand and dips them into the tin. The coconut sticks and she sucks it off, finger by finger, with great relish

Café Daphne You're just in time to add a bit of style to the lunch menu. (*She picks up a blank menu and a pencil*) Now. What can you do with this: two pork chops, fried potatoes, sprouts and coconut tarts with custard.

Café Daphne stands by, ready to write, while Brenda thinks

Brenda "A perfect pair of pork chops, served with newly dug up hand-cut fried potatoes ... and sprouts specially brought over from Brussels."

Café Daphne writes rapidly. Brenda leans over to inspect

Brenda I think it's two esses and one el, Café Daphne. (*Pause*) And tarts sprinkled with magical coconut snowflakes ... served beneath an avalanche of golden custard.

Café Daphne You're a real little gen us, so you are. Every time I display one of your menus my clientele have to fight their way through the crowd of gawpers gathered outside.

Brenda (*trying to hide intense pleasure*) Really?

Café Daphne On my word of honour. Here, sign your name to it.

Brenda Oh I better not, Café Daphne, for fear my Granny would find out.

Café Daphne Is she still going round saying I'm a danger to public morals? I was your Aunty Peace's best friend till your Granny put a ban on me. But sure the Clearys' were always full of themselves—just because you live in a three storey house doesn't mean you're closer to heaven.

The Voice of Enrico Caruso is heard off, as if upstairs, singing loudly and clearly in a rich tenor voice, to the melody of "Come Back To Sorrento"

Caruso (*singing*)   I would like my morning tea dear
I would like my morning tea dear
I would like my morning tea dear
I would like my morning tea

Brenda and Café Daphne are thrilled. Café Daphne pretends to be cross. She walks to the exit and calls, as if up the stairs

Café Daphne Will you shush up there and stop disgracing me and I expecting the lunch time trade. Morning tea and it half past twelve. If you want tea, sing yourself down the stairs and get it yourself! (*To Brenda*) I've had to train myself to be very firm with visiting artistes. Otherwise they walk all over you. But this one's gorgeous! Great style—real showbiz. He'll be harin' down for his tea any minute now, Brenda. Would you ever mind the cafe for me while I nip over the road?

Brenda I will. But Café Daphne ...

Café Daphne (*removing her apron*) Mmmm?

Brenda I was just wondering if you'd had a chance to read it, like.
Café Daphne (*finding her string bag*) I certainly have.
Brenda Was it any good? Did you like it?
Café Daphne (*heading for the exit*) No.

Brenda is disappointed. Café Daphne turns back, all smiles

I didn't *like* it—I *loved* it, so I did. When that horse started dying before he had a chance to enjoy the bit of sugar, I cried my eyes out. And the snow falling. And the bell tolling. Sure the gloom of it would make a rock weep. Haven't I always told you you're a born writer, Brenda Barnes. Remember now I said that, and when you're world famous, don't forget your pal Café Daphne.
Brenda (*fervently*) I'll never forget you, Café Daphne, and when my first book is published, I'll tell everybody the way you helped me.

Caruso is heard off. He sings to the melody of "La donna e mobile"

Caruso (*singing*)   I hear a voice below
                          Some one I do not know
                          I am now coming down
                          In my new dressing-gown.

Daphne exits

Caruso enters. He wears a flamboyant dressing-gown over trousers and carries an artificial flower

Caruso (*in a phoney Italian accent*) So. The stranger is a pretty senorita. (*He gives Brenda the flower*) Whatsa you name? Whatsa the matter—catta gotta you tongue? Whatsa you name?
Brenda (*shyly*) Brenda Barnes.

Caruso helps himself to tea from the urn, ready milked

Caruso And do you know who I am?
Brenda I do.
Caruso Who am I then?
Brenda (*mumbling*) The Voice of Enrico Caruso.
Caruso (*sternly*) Louder please. Lift you chin when you speak. And separate you teeth. Now: loud and clear: Whom do you have the honour of addressing?
Brenda (*loudly and clearly*) The Voice of Enrico Caruso.
Caruso Is better. Mucha better. Tell me, you seen yet my wonderful performance at the Town Hall?
Brenda Not yet. But my Aunty Peace has, and she sent a message to Café Daphne asking could she get us a few more free tickets.
Caruso Is no more free tickets. People they come for miles to hear The Voice. How many times you get a chance to hear a tenor so magnificent? This is the twenty second town on my national tour. Wherever I go I am the news—big news. Tell me you—what you Mamma and Pappa saying about The Voice of Enrico Caruso? Tell me. (*He ladles a heap of sugar into his cup*) I like to hear what the people they have to say.

Brenda My mother and father are in England. But I'll be going over any day now. I'm just here on holidays with my grandmother and my aunt.

Caruso So what they say?

Brenda . . . nothing.

Caruso They musta say *something*. I am the talk of the town. Speak, child, speak.

Brenda My Granny says if you were a great fella you'd be staying at a big hotel, not Café Daphne's. Aunty Peace says you're great gas but the real Caruso would choke if I heard you. Bella Rafferty says—

Caruso Gratias. Stop. Is enough. And what *you* think of me, pretty Brenda?

Brenda Would you like more tea?

Caruso puts down his cup

Caruso Come here, senorita. Today you lucky day. Because today I give you a chance to kiss a great celebrity.

Brenda Ah, it's all right. Don't worry.

Caruso taps his cheek, inviting Brenda to kiss the spot. Brenda looks anxiously towards the exit

Caruso Quickly! Or you lose your chance.

Caruso moves closer to Brenda and extends his cheek. She reluctantly leans towards him to kiss him. At the last second he turns his head and plants a kiss on her mouth. He prolongs the kiss by grasping her head and bending her over backwards. She freezes with fright

Café Daphne enters with her shopping

Café Daphne Sweet Saint Jude! What's this!

Caruso (*losing his Italian accent*) Take it easy, Café Daphne. 'Twas just a little kiss. The child wanted to kiss The Voice of Enrico Caruso.

Café Daphne (*suspiciously*) Do you ask him to kiss you, Brenda Barnes?

Caruso She did—bold as brass. I offered my cheek like, and didn't she swivel her head at the last minute. I'll tell you now, I'm glad you came back when you did, pet—

Café Daphne Don't sweet talk me, you deceitful little scut. And we unofficially engaged.

Caruso (*resuming his Italian accent*) Excuse me ladies. I musta prepare myself. I have a mationeé at halfa pasta two. Arrivederci!

Caruso exits speedily

Café Daphne (*very coldly*) What do you mean by enticing my fella like that, Brenda Barnes? You've always been too forward. You're like the rest of the Clearys, going around thinking you're a cut above. Well I don't want to see you hanging around here ever again. (*She snatches the flower from Brenda*)

Brenda (*very upset*) But he pointed to his cheek, Café Daphne.

Café Daphne (*close to tears*) All innocence till my back was turned, you sneaky girl. You've your whole life to find fellas of your own. And me like a gom trusting you, thinking we were pals. Here—(*She rummages angrily in the bottom shelf of her trolley and finds Brenda's notebook*) take your stuff and get out!

Café Daphne holds out the notebook. Brenda takes it reluctantly, then turns away, trying to keep up a brave front. Café Daphne, her face stoney, pushes her trolley R. *Both Brenda and Café Daphne pause, look back at each other. Brenda is hopeful as Café Daphne seems to relent*

> *Caruso is heard off, singing cheerfully*

Caruso (*off*) "Kiss me, honey honey kiss me, thrill me, honey honey, thrill me . . ."

> *The song motivates Café Daphne to exit stormily* R

> *Brenda, last hope gone, exits sadly,* L

Caruso's song is taken over by a non-vocal version of the song

> *Bella Rafferty cha-cha's on for scene seven*

SCENE 7

1953. The Postman Scene. The kitchen of Granny Cleary's Galway House

There's a holy picture, an upholstered wing-backed chair, a long wooden bench, a hanging laundry rack

Bella cha-cha's around the room, dancing to "Kiss Me Honey Honey, Kiss Me". She absolutely adores herself and makes a big number out of it

Peace, aged thirty-five enters. She is wearing a dress. She glares at Bella

Peace Who invited you, Bella Rafferty? I wish you'd have the manners to knock before you just walk in here without as much as a by-your-leave. This is a private house, not a dance hall.
Bella New dress, *Miss* Cleary? Now if I had that I'd wear it with a lovely big wide belt and black patent slingbacks.
Peace And look as tarty as you, is it? You're a disgrace, going round half-dressed, and it broad daylight.

Peace turns her back and Bella sticks out her tongue

> *Brenda, aged thirteen, comes in excitedly. She is hoping for a letter and has crossed her fingers, arms and legs, for luck*

Brenda The post is here! The post!
Bella Will you stop twisting yourself in knots, Brenda Barnes. If you haven't got a letter no amount of crossing will make any difference!
Peace Arra, leave her alone, and she dying for her letter from her mother.

> *Michael the Postman enters with his satchel of mail and a bundle of letters in his hand*

Michael 'Morning.
Peace Ah, there you are Michael, come in, come in. Mammy—the post!

Granny enters at a snail's pace, using a walking stick

Granny More haste, less speed, Peace. This damp weather stiffens me up and slows me down.

While Brenda hops around impatiently, Granny finally arrives at her chair and settles herself in. Michael hands her the letters

Musha sit down Michael, while I put on my glasses.
Bella (*flirting*) Sit here next to me, Michael. Is this a special delivery, then?

Michael takes a seat on the bench

Michael Indeed it is, Bella. The like I've never seen before and I fifteen years a postman.

Granny has three letters. She holds one up to the light. It is airmail stickered and bulky. Granny rattles it, smells it, then puts it aside. She selects a less important-looking one and opens it. Her lips move as she reads silently

Brenda Anything for me?
Michael Indeed there is, Brenda. The like I've never seen before and I fifteen years a postman.

Brenda uncrosses everything

Bella Sure you told us that a minute ago.
Michael (*shyly*) Fifteen years and a minute, so.
Granny (*scanning the letter*) Your cousin Kevin is cycling down from Dublin and his mother wants to know can he stay for a few days in preparation for the journey back.
Peace (*all scorn*) Cycling a hundred and thirty miles. He's always been daft, that fella.
Granny The new baby arrived on the fifteenth ... 'Twas a girl. She called it Myrna and now she has the full set of Three Wise Men—
Michael (*to Granny*) Sure it's none of my business, but what does she mean by that?
Granny The gifts the three wise men brought to Bethlehem: Gold, Frankincense and Myrrh.

Michael continues to look blank

Peace My auntie called her kids after the gifts: Goldie, Frankie and the new one, Myrna.
Michael (*understanding dawning*) Goldie, Frankie and Myrna. Well, isn't that a good one. I've never heard the like of that, and I fifteen—
Peace Go on Mammy!
Granny They've had a lot of rain ... Kevin can sleep in the sitting room ... Indeed he *won't* sleep in the sitting room and it for visitors. He can have your bed, Peace; you can go next door to Rafferty's. Will that be all right, Bella?

Bella Of course it will, Mrs Cleary. Or Peace can stay here and Kevin can sleep in my bed. (*She smirks at Peace*)
Granny (*missing the innuendo*) That's nice of you, love. Now let's see: (*She reads on silently*)
Michael (*still marvelling*) Myrrhh-na! Well, aren't ye an interesting family? Tell me now why Peace is called Peace?

Peace rolls her eyes; it's clear she's often been asked before

Peace Because I was born the day the war ended.
Bella World War *One*.
Michael We'll always know your age so. You won't be able to let on you're younger than you are with a name like that!

Peace ignores Michael. Bella is delighted. Granny carefully folds the letter and puts it back in its envelope

Brenda Can I have mine now, Granny? Can I have mine?

Granny takes the important-looking letter and examines it thoroughly. It has a nice red seal on it, lots of stamps and an airmail sticker

Michael (*to Brenda*) Whisht now till you see.
Granny Have you a penpal in Italy, atall atall?
Bella }
Peace } (*together*) Italy?
Michael (*not impressed, he already knew*) Italy!
Granny Search your mind and be sure. Did you by any chance drop a line in that direction?
Brenda (*embarrassed*) I did.

Michael slaps his thigh delightedly. Bella also slaps his thigh. He is embarrassed

Granny And may we ask to whom you wrote, or is it a secret?
Brenda (*shyly*) To . . . to His Holiness Pope Pius.

They all gasp. Granny hastily crosses herself

Bella (*amazed*) What the hell did you write to the Pope for? Sorry, Mrs Cleary.
Brenda Did he write back? Is that for me, that letter?
Michael It is—and there's something round and hard in it. I'd say it was a big, thick coin.

Brenda reaches for the letter

Granny (*officiously withdrawing the letter*) 'Tis addressed to you, Brenda, but as head of the Legion of Mary I feel 'twould be better if I opened it for you, and you a child.
Brenda (*meekly*) All right.

Granny opens the letter with utter reverence. A large gold medal on a fine chain drops out. Peace, Michael, Bella and Brenda drop to the floor and remain in a clutch at Granny's feet, poring over it

Bella Jesus, Mary and Joseph, he's sent her a solid gold medal of himself.
Peace Don't touch it, and his Holiness's fingerprints still warm upon it!
Michael Didn't I tell you it was something the size of a coin? Wasn't it true
for me! A medal, and Brenda barely over her confirmation.

*Meantime Granny has been reading the letter. She suddenly shrieks and drops
it as if it's on fire. She grasps Brenda's ear and pulls her to a kneeling position*

Granny Sacred Heart! What did you write to His Holiness Pope Pius. The
Head of the Catholic Church?
Brenda Nothing.
Granny Answer me or I'll brain you. What did you write, you ungrateful
brat, and you living here free of charge, you little scut!
Bella I bet she wrote begging for the medal. Gimme the letter till I see.

*Everybody makes a dive for the letter, but Bella gets it. She jumps up and holds
it aloft, reading it silently to herself. After a few seconds she gasps*

Holy . . . Mary . . . Mother of God.

Bella sits down, dramatically distraught. Peace grabs the letter and scans it

Peace (*tragically*) She's us disgraced.

Michael removes the letter from Peace's numb fingers

Michael Sure whatever's in it, it's a miracle to get a letter from the Vatican.

He looks around, decides to read the letter and begins with great confidence

"Dear Brenda. His Holiness thanks you for your letter and has asked me
to convey the following in respect of your five intentions. *One*: the matter
of you being dumped in Galway while your parents are off galli-a-vating:
This period of separation will strengthen the bonds of love between you.
Patience is a great virtue."
Granny (*through gritted teeth*) The rip. The little rip.
Michael "*Two*: The matter of Bella Rafferty's seduction of the young man
preparing for the priesthood: This should be referred at once to your
parish priest . . ."
Bella I'll never be able to show my face in the Vatican. (*She arranges herself
tragically, but sexily as always*).
Michael *Three*: The matter of your Grandmother's lack of personal hy-
giene. His Holiness will certainly not overlook this matter in his prayers,
but the fact that many elder-elly people prefer not to bathe daily must be
taken into consideration . . .
Granny (*sorrowfully*) A guest in my house. My own daughter's child.
Michael *Four*: The matter of your Aunty Peace's thick glasses. God in his
wisdom has seen fit to endow her with poor eyesight, but this does not
mean that he intended her to lead a lonely life. Many married Catholics
wear glasses.
Peace (*standing*) I don't feel at all well, Mammy. I think I'm going to faint.
Granny Don't be working yourself up, Peace. *Sit down.*

Peace sits

You might as well read on, Michael, you know all our business now anyway.

Michael (*nervously*) Will I go on, Brenda?

Granny
Peace }(*together, snapping*) Read on!
Bella

Michael *Five*: The matter of a three-speed black and gold junior bicycle for Christmas: His Holiness cannot concern himself with requests for worlddilly goods of this kind, but advises that personal prayer makes all things possible. The enclosed medallion—

Brenda makes a move to pick up the medallion but Granny quickly covers it with her stick or her foot

—has been blessed by His Holiness. Signed on behalf of Pope Pius, by Mon-sig-nor Flaherty, Vatican Secretarial Staff. P.S. (*He marvels at the next bit, pointing excitedly up the road*) Former-elly Martin Flaherty of Raleigh Row! Regards to all in Galway!

Granny Isn't it a great day for us all. Michael? A great day for discovering a Judas among us. Let us pray for guidance through the period of trial and disgrace that lies ahead. On your knees!

Granny stands and slaps at both Bella and Peace. They kneel. Granny tries to kneel on her armchair, facing her Sacred Heart picture. She manages one leg, then gets stuck. She slaps at Michael. Startled, he gives her a leg up. She knocks the cap from his head. He kneels with the others

(*Forcefully*) Our Father who art in heaven hallowed be Thy name. Thy kingdom come Thy will be done on earth as it is in heaven.

Peace ⎫ (*together,*   Give us this day our daily bread and forgive
Bella ⎬*raggedly*   us our trespasses as we forgive them who
Michael ⎭ *at top*   trespass against us and lead us not into
       speed   temptation but deliver us from evil Amen.

Granny Hail Mary full of grace the Lord is with Thee. Blessed art Thou among women and blessed is the fruit of Thy womb Jesus.

Peace
Bella   }   Holy Mary mother of God pray for us sinners now
Michael   and at the hour of our death Amen.

Brenda stealthily picks up and puts on her medallion, and opens the third letter. The prayers are repeated as required while she scans it

Granny Hail Mary full of grace the Lord is with Thee. Blessed art Thou among women and blessed is the fruit of Thy womb Jesus.

Brenda (*very excited*) My Mammy and Daddy have sent for me! Here's the ticket and all. I'm going to England at the end of term. And I've a baby brother (*She reads*) "He was christened Peter but Daddy changed it to Ted". And my Dad's like a new man. He's got a job in an aeroplane factory that makes jet engines. Here's the ticket and everything. I'm going to England at last!

Granny, still kneeling, throws back her head and raises her arms in thanks

Granny Our prayers have been answered!

Cheerful church bells and music herald the next scene

> *Granny and the others strike their props, still muttering prayers and responses*

Brenda produces a skipping rope and begins to skip briskly

SCENE 8

1953. The Bicycle Scene. A street in Galway

There's a section of ivy-covered canal wall, L

Brenda, aged thirteen, is skipping with a rope

Kevin enters, pushing his bicycle. He is bent over. His muscles have contracted after his marathon cycle across Ireland. He can barely walk. His speech is slow and grave. He wears a cap and bicycle clips

Kevin Good morning, Brenda.

Brenda (*stopping her skipping for a moment*) Oh, there you are Kevin. I thought you were going to stay in bed for ever—and I wouldn't blame you, after cycling a hundred and thirty miles.

Kevin I hear you're off to England then Brenda?

Brenda (*airily resuming her skipping*) I am. Sure my Dad's desperate to see me and we apart nearly three years. My father's a new man. As a matter of fact he's just invented the jet engine. Which part of you hurts the most Kevin, your arms or your legs?

Kevin (*after considering*) I'd say my back's the worst off at the present. Legs second worst, arms third worst.

Brenda (*stopping her skipping*) Your bike still looks brand new though. You'd think 'twould be filthy after being on the road so long.

Brenda handles the bike. Kevin kindly but firmly removes her hands

Kevin I cleaned it last night before I seized up. I'd say you could keep a bike looking brand new forever by cleaning it daily. That's what I intend to do. I saved for this for nearly four years. It costs me eleven pounds. Ten, nineteen and six to be exact.

Brenda I'm getting a ladies' one for Christmas by arrangement with the Vatican. I wrote asking the Pope for a few things and got a letter back and a gold medallion in it.

Kevin I heard about that before I left Dublin. Not to mention Athlone, Ballinasloe and Athenry. I'm not surprised you can't wait to go. Sure you've disgraced the name of the family. And what's all this talk about wanting to be English? What's wrong with being Irish?

Brenda I want to be calm like the English. And speak in a lovely loud clear voice and have a king to look up to and all.
Kevin The King of England died nearly a year ago. Did ye not hear in Galway?
Brenda You're a liar, Kevin Cleary.
Kevin Indeed I'm not. So you'll have to settle for a queen. His nibs's daughter Princess Elizabeth will be taking the throne. You ought to write one of your letters to her, asking would she give us back the six counties.
Brenda (*skipping again*) Why would I bother writing when I'm going over? (*She shakes her head at his stupidity*) Anyway, nothing I do is any of your business.
Kevin (*looking at her admiringly*) Did you . . . did you ever get a kiss from a fella, Brenda?
Brenda (*smiling despite herself*) Indeed I wouldn't be bothered.
Kevin Will I give you one, while you're still Irish?
Brenda You will not . . . unless . . .
Kevin Unless what?
Brenda (*stopping her skipping*) Unless you give me a ride on your bike.
Kevin Not a chance. Sure I've nothing more precious than my bike.

Brenda skips again at a slow, seductive pace

Kevin is now longing to kiss her. He makes his decision, and turns his stiff body towards her

Kevin All right so.

Brenda drops the rope instantly and wipes her mouth. After glancing around, she closes her eyes and allows herself to be kissed briefly. Their noses get in the way. Kevin's limbs twitch with excitement. Brenda pulls away and grabs the bike. She jumps on and cycles around, wobbling. Kevin is very anxious. He hobbles after her

Be careful now, Brenda. I thought you were more experienced. Mind! Mind now the way you're steering.
Brenda (*cycling offstage*) Don't worry, Kev, I'll be careful. This is great gas!

Brenda exits

Kevin (*watching from* CS) Keep well away from the canal wall, Brenda. Keep to the middle of the path. Mind, mind!

There's a scream and a small crash followed by silence. Kevin remains frozen

Brenda enters slowly, pushing the bike backwards.

Brenda wheels the bike to Kevin. There's no sign of any damage. Kevin stares at it. Brenda glances around nervously

(*Softly*) 'Tis chipped and bent.
Brenda Only the mud-guard Kevin. Sure you'd need a microscope to see it.
Kevin (*as if entranced*) 'Tis chipped and bent. So 'tis no use to me now. I don't want it if 'tis chipped and bent. Why would I, when I had it brand

new? 'Tis ruined now and that's all about it. (*He takes the bike from Brenda and slowly pushes it off. To himself, in a monotone*) A chipped, bent bike isn't the same as a bike that isn't chipped and bent. Sure there's no comparison at all, wouldn't anyone understand that.

Kevin exits

Brenda (*looking off; horrified*) What are you doing? Janey Mack, don't do that Kevin. 'Tis only the mud-guard! Don't, Kevin, don't!

Brenda freezes. There's a splash. Kevin enters slowly after a moment. He has removed his cap and now twists it in his hands.

Brenda backs away from him

Kevin (*with immense gloom*) 'Tis safe as a dead sailor now, in its grave at the bottom of the canal. May its soul and the souls of the faithful departed, rest in peace, Amen.

Brenda (*very distressed*) You're an *ejit* Kevin Cleary! You're like everyone else around here. You're all touched. Mental! The way a person wouldn't know where they are with you. Well, I'm different entirely. That's why I don't fit in, and I'm glad I don't. I'm going and I'm never coming back. Never! So you can throw *yourself* in the canal for all I care!

Brenda looks around for her skipping rope, locates it and is about to resume her skipping when Kevin, ignoring her completely, begins to sing a heartbroken lament for his lost bicycle. It is the only 'holy' song Kevin can think of. Brenda's anger fades as she listens

Kevin (*softly and brokenly*) O Danny boy, the pipes the pipes are calling. From glen to glen and down the mountain side. The summer's gone and all the flowers are dying, tis you, tis you, must go and I must bide.

Slow fade to Black-out, or CURTAIN

An orchestrated, instrumental version of Danny Boy *fades in on the correct phrase and swells majestically*

ACT II

SCENE 1

1953. The Workhouse Scene. Coronation Year in London

As the CURTAIN *rises we hear a perky instrumental version of "Rule Brittania". Mr Mullen, the landlord, is supervising the departure of the Barnes family from his apartment house, the interior of which is represented by the wing. Brenda, aged thirteen, is sitting mournfully on her suitcase,* DL, *holding her statue of the Madonna and teddy-bear. Desmond, aged forty-three, rocks a large, rather grand pram. He is clearly attached to the baby in it. Bridie, aged forty, wearing a coat and headscarf, makes frequent trips to and fro with a case and various parcels, which she puts on, or hangs from, the pram till it becomes a misshapen vehicle for all her worldly goods. She mutters and sighs as she toils*

Mr Mullen No hard feelings then, Des? I mean, you've got to understand that overcrowding is illegal here in England. I think it's something to do with the number of toilets per square foot. Sure I'd have no objection personally, but amn't I renting the place meself, Des, and not supposed to be subletting atall atall.

Desmond (*wheedling*) A couple of weeks. An extension of a couple of weeks. I've always been a good tenant.

Mr Mullen Well, I don't know about that, Des. I thought I was letting that room to a bachelor. Next thing your missus moves in, and before I can catch my bloody breath, she's multiplied by two! But the arrival of that big kid was the last straw. Were you planning to sleep in shifts, were you? Ah now, a fella has to draw the line somewhere, Des.

Desmond (*looking at Brenda*) The minute she turned up everything went wrong. I'd my wife, and my boy, and myself. Time for a bit of peace and prosperity, I thought. And then her nibs arrived.

The baby begins to cry

Bridie comes on with a baby bottle and gives it to Desmond

Desmond puts it under the hood of the pram, clucking and cooing at the baby. The crying stops abruptly

Mr Mullen All set, then?

Bridie (*with dignity*) You've no right to put us out like this, Mr Mullen. It's impossible to find family accommodation, as well you know—

Desmond Will you stop whinging, Bridie. We're out now, like it or not.

Mr Mullen (*very cheerfully*) Well. I'll say goodbye then. (*Pause*) Goodbye.

Desmond and Mr Mullen shake hands

Mr Mullen exits

Desmond picks up a suitcase

Desmond You'll have to put yourselves at the mercy of the British Government. Sure they love showing off how charitable they are—and they in great humour over the Coronation. Just present yourselves at one of those Rest Centres for the homeless, and we'll go at the top of the list for a nice council flat. (*He leans into the pram, pulling loving faces at the baby*)

Bridie (*incredulously*) And where will you be, while me and the children are living it up in the workhouse? Back in the pub, spending money on strangers, I suppose?

Desmond (*irrationally furious*) I'll be looking for a job! Now do what I tell you or beJesus I'll lose me temper! Haven't I enough on my mind without you nagging away like a squeaking chalk! Just trust me—I know what I'm doing. They'll be more sentimental about a woman and children on their own. Go on now, before it gets dark. When they fix you up leave a message with Mullen.

Desmond exits, striding off without a backward glance

The baby lets out a single wail. Brenda watches Desmond exit

Bridie (*restrained*) Sweet Holy Mary, hear my prayer. *God* hear my prayer! ... if there is a God ... God forgive me. (*She crosses herself hastily*) Come on Brenda.

Brenda Where are we going to go, Mam? I still feel a bit seasick from the boat ... (*She brightens*) Could we go to a hotel in a lovely London taxi?

Bridie Ahh shut up, Brenda, when you know well he left us without a penny. I wish now I'd left you in Galway a bit longer.

Brenda I wish I'd never been born!

Bridie Just grow up quick and get a job. Look at us—like tinkers, but without a caravan. Come on so, before it gets dark.

The entourage moves slowly around the stage, in a tight little unit. An enamel teapot clangs mournfully as the pram is wheeled. On arrival at the Rest Centre, Bridie steps forward and mimes an echoing knock, as if on a huge workhouse door. After a pause, we hear the turning of a massive key, the squeak of a door being opened. Bridie clutches Brenda nervously

A shaft of light falls onto the stage from the wing as the "door" opens

Two terribly English social workers, Mrs Geeny and Mrs Brown enter, carrying clipboards

Mrs Geeny (*kindly but firmly*) Are you the party who telephoned? Do hurry up dear, we don't like receiving after four, it makes us frightfully late. I'm Mrs Geeny and my colleague is Mrs Brown. Come come, sign here if you would.

Bridie (*faintly*) What am I signing?

Mrs Brown Simply that you are quite without funds, quite destitute

Mrs Geeny—That you understand you are entering a *Rest Centre*, and after a period of not less than three months and not exceeding twelve months, you will qualify to be transferred to a *Halfway House*, for a period of not less than twelve months and not exceeding two years

Mrs Brown —That although every effort will be made to find you London County Council accommodation, you are requested to make every effort to find *private* accommodation, thus relieving the burden on the state.

Mrs Geeny —That you and your children are prepared to undertake whatever chores the hostel matron sees fit.

Mrs Brown That you understand the Rest Centre is *exclusively* for women and children and no males can be admitted at any time other than prescribed visiting hours.

Mrs Geeny (*getting faster*) That you'll report the presence of lice, venereal disease and any other contagious conditions to the Visiting Health Officer.

Bridie draws Brenda close

Mrs Brown No liquor to be consumed on the premises—

Mrs Geeny Rest Centre not responsible for theft—

Mrs Brown (*almost gabbling*) No cooking in the dormitory—

Mrs Geeny Do sign in dear, we haven't got all night.

Bridie signs the documents on the clipboards and the two social workers usher the entourage off stage. As Bridie exits, chin up and dignified, we hear the music of "Land of Hope and Glory".

> *They all exit*

SCENE 2

1953. The Stilts Scene. The Rest Centre's bleak playground, decorated with Coronation bunting

Brenda, aged thirteen, carries in and sits on an old crate. She thinks intently, then writes in her notebook

Trevor and Di are heard clanking about offstage

Di (*off*) 'Ere Trev, let's play steppin' in and out the crate.

Trevor (*off*) Oh, yeah!

> *Trevor and Di, both aged about thirteen, enter on homemade stilts. These are made from crude wood, with the footpiece about eighteen inches above the ground. The stilts are decorated with metal bottle caps, bits of bunting, pictures of Royals and labels from containers such as Ovaltine, Oxo etc. The children are shabby and scruffy*

Di (*as she enters*) And whoever falls off first is a silly little sod, right?

Trevor Yeah!
Di (*spotting Brenda*) Hey you!
Brenda What?
Di Don't you "what" us. You're sitting on our crate.
Trevor Yeah. Get your arse off of our crate.
Brenda (*standing*) Sorry. Sure I didn't know it was yours.
Di Oh no. Not another batch of bleeding Irish. Jesus wept, the Rest
  Centre's full of them.
Trevor Why don't you lot stay put in the bogs.

Brenda remains silent

Di Oy! My mate Trevor spoke to you, girl. You better answer him unless
  you want a stilt around your ear.
Brenda We've got a right to come here. You've got our six counties, in
  Ulster.
Di That don't mean you can come here and sponge off of us. 'Ere I hope
  you've got proper respect for our Queen?
Brenda I have.
Trevor Well you better have because she's our sovereign lady.
Di If she come in here right this minute, what would you do, Paddywack?
Brenda I'd ... I'd say hello to her.

Trevor and Di laugh coarsely at this

Di Say hello to her, would you? Like hell you would. You'd bloody fall flat
  on your face and worship the ground she walked on, that's what you'd
  do, girl.
Brenda Indeed I would not.
Trevor (*squeaking with outrage*) I beg your pardon?
Brenda Catholics don't worship anybody except the Three Divine Persons,
  The Blessed Virgin Mary and the Saints. We're not allowed.
Di (*looking down at Brenda*) You know something Bog-face, I don't like
  you.
Trevor (*imitating Di*) Nor do I.

They climb off their stilts and they position themselves either side of Brenda

Di You want to live in England, right? And that means you're going to act
  like an English person, right?
Brenda What do you mean?
Di I mean you're gonna treat the Queen with respect, being as she's your
  sovereign lady. So you're gonna say after me "the Queen is more
  important than what the Virgin Mary is".
Brenda No.
Trevor We ain't joking, girl. You better say it quick before me and Di lose
  our temper. (*He nudges Brenda with a stilt*)
Brenda Sure a Catholic could never say a thing like that. The Queen is very
  ladylike and everything, but the Virgin Mary—Sure there's no comparison, really there isn't ... (*She tries to escape*)

The children block her whichever way she turns

Di ⎱ *(together)*   The Queen is more important than what the Virgin
Trevor ⎰   Mary is.

Brenda I can't say that. I wouldn't be a Catholic if I said a thing like that. A
person would go straight to hell.

Di ⎱ *(together)*   The Queen is more important than what the Virgin
Trevor ⎰   Mary is.

Brenda *(scared)* I can't. 'Twould be a mortal sin.

Di ⎱ *(together)*   The Queen is more important than what the Virgin
Trevor ⎰   Mary is. The Queen is more important than what the
                          Virgin Mary is.

Brenda tries to escape through the bars formed by the stilts

The Queen is more important than what the Virgin Mary is: The Queen—

*They use the stilts to force Brenda to the ground, continuing the chant. There's
a huge clap of thunder followed by a lengthy flash of lightning. Brenda looks at
the sky in wonderment*

Di *(shrieking)* 'Ere! It's gonna pour down! Let's go indoors.
Trevor *(shrieking)* Ta ta Paddywack. See you tomorrow.

Di and Trevor run off

*Brenda remains crumpled on the floor until they've gone. She continues to look
up at the sky and smiles radiantly. She gives a shaky little wave of the hand
towards heaven, in thanks*

Brenda exits

Scene 3

1956. The Racing Scene. On open ground at Epsom Racecourse

*Desmond, aged forty-six, enters and surveys the scene through binoculars. We
hear the thunder of hooves and horses snorting, the distant roar of a crowd.
The sound grows, peaks, then fades as it passes Desmond. He tears up a racing
ticket and puts the pieces in his pocket*

*Brenda, aged fifteen, enters carrying a folded tartan rug and a firm straw
shopping basket*

Brenda *(cheerfully)* Here I am, Dad. I bet you thought you'd lost me.

Desmond ignores her. Brenda looks around for a suitable place to settle

This looks like a nice place, Daddy. Would this be OK? Or we could go
over there, but I think here is more even and cleaner for the rug, Dad.
Desmond For Jesus sake, will you stop whisheting on about where we're
going to sit. There's no difference between one piece of freezing cold grass

and another. We're here for the races. The picnic aspect of the thing is of secondary importance. (*He surveys the course*)

We hear the crackle of a loudspeaker. Followed by an announcement

Announcer "Jockey changes. Thundercat, number seven, will now be ridden by Damian Kelleher. Aubrey's Luck, number three, will now be ridden by Peter Hodes."

Desmond makes notes on his racecard

Brenda Will we sit here, then?

Desmond glares at her. Brenda hastily spreads out the rug

(*Chattering away*) There we are—lovely and comfy if you get tired standing up, Daddy. Or even if you don't get tired and *don't* feel like sitting, it's nice to look down and see a rug spread out. Sure there's no such thing as a picnic without a rug, Daddy. (*She takes a flask, two greaseproof-wrapped packages and her notebook out of the basket, cheerfully whistling "Happy Birthday"*)

Desmond (*looking through the binoculars*) Stop whistling, Brenda. I cannot stand a whistling woman.

Brenda Sorry Daddy. And thanks again for bringing me to the races, Dad. It's the best birthday present I've ever had. The best ever. Thanks again, Daddy. And I hope you're not too disappointed that Ted couldn't come, but I suppose they don't want small kids running around, frightening the horses. Anyway, I'm writing a little poem to commemorate the day. What rhymes with races Dad? "A father and daughter went to the races . . ."

Desmond (*lowering his glasses*) How about: "She should've stayed home where a daughter's place is". Now will you hush up till I hear the odds. How can a person hear your man doing his commentary with you gabbing away.

Brenda puts her notebook away and busies herself with the picnic things. Then she tries out various positions of relaxation, mostly based on fifties' model poses. She has difficulty in getting comfortable, finds bumpy things under the rug, etc

Brenda Isn't it great the way everything is turning out. Dad? (*She counts her blessings on her fingers*) You like your new job, and our family lives in a lovely little flat, with a television set, a fridge, a pressure cooker, a spin drier, an Electrolux—

Desmond Look: When you've got a bet on a horse you've got to *will* it home with the muscles of your stomach. I've a fiver each way on *Aubrey's Luck*. A long shot, but in with a chance—*if* I'm allowed to concentrate. The way you're going on is why men rarely take women to the races. Too much talking and distraction and fussing about refreshments. (*Pause*) So where's the grub?

Brenda pats the rug. After glancing around, Desmond sits

Brenda The big one is ham sandwiches and the small one is fruit cake. I think we should start with the sandwiches and keep the fruit cake for dessert.

Desmond Is the fruit cake buttered?

Brenda I don't know.

Desmond It bloody well better be buttered. Time and time again I tell your mother I like a bit of butter on my fruit cake. Time and time again she pretends she's forgotten to put it on.

Brenda I suppose she thinks it's rich enough as it is, Dad. Better for you, like.

Desmond *I'll* decide what's good and bad for me. Your mother never stops dictating to me what I eat and how I'll eat it.

Brenda Ah well, I bet you anything it's buttered. I mean she'd be bound to butter it on my birthday, wouldn't she Dad?

The race and commentary begin and are heard distantly

Desmond Well, she better have, or you can start folding your picnic rug. I like a bit of fruit cake in a butter sandwich, God help me. Jesus, is that too much to ask? A bit of butter between two slices of fruit cake. (*He picks up and begins to unfold the greaseproof paper wrapped around the fruit cake, stopping to look towards the race track from time to time*)

Brenda's tension mounts as the racing commentary speeds up and becomes more urgent. She watches as Desmond continues to unwrap the paper unbearably slowly. Feeling observed, Desmond turns his back and proceeds with his task. Brenda sits frozen, awaiting the verdict. The commentary becomes frenetic and the crowd begins to roar. Desmond tosses the package aside, jumps up and positions his binoculars

Aubrey's Luck! Come on *Aubrey's Luck!*

Brenda stealthily reaches for the package. She holds it in the palm of her outstretched left hand and uses her right hand to bend back the wrapping, exposing a thick slab of dark fruit cake comprised of four fat slices, one on top of the other. As Desmond continues to root for Aubrey's Luck, Brenda closes her eyes and chants

Brenda (*louder and louder*) Let it be buttered. Let it be buttered. LET IT BE BUTTERED. LET IT BE BUTTERED.

Almost too scared to look, she lifts off a slice of fruit cake and finds it thickly buttered. At the same moment, Desmond's horse passes the post in the winning position

Desmond It's *Aubrey's Luck*!

Brenda It's buttered!

Brenda and Desmond yell with delight and in the excitement of the moment, they grab for each other. Brenda gets carried away and jumps up, childishly wrapping her legs around Desmond

The background noise dies down. Brenda and Desmond disentangle themselves. Desmond brushes at his clothes but is too pleased with his win to be irritable

Desmond (*in excellent spirits*) Come on! Let's go and collect our winnings!

Brenda, all smiles, puts the picnic things away. She hums Happy Birthday *in a cheerful and witty sort of way, without the slightest sentiment. She and Desmond fold the rug*

Brenda (*humming, no lyric*) Happy birthday to you, happy birthday to you, happy birthday dear . . . (*She stops, hoping Desmond will join in*)
Desmond (*humming as Brenda did, no lyric*) . . . BREN-DA
Brenda   } (*together,*
Desmond } *no lyric*) Happy birthday to you.
Desmond (*after a pause*) Come on, then.

   Desmond strides off cheerfully

Brenda, her face radiant, pauses to look downstage for a moment, then follows

SCENE 4

1962. The Madison Scene. A small bedsit in London

Di, aged twenty pushes on a large, pink chest of drawers. Items of clothing bulge out of its drawers. On top, there's a lamp and a small record player, on which we hear a tinny version of The Madison (Ray Ellington). Di is wearing very sixties clothes and bright pink stiletto heeled shoes

Di exits dancing and returns with a chair.

She practises the Madison, describing the steps (substitute appropriate lines according to choreography)

Di Step touch, step touch, back criss cross touch (*Repeat as needed*)

   Brenda, aged twenty, enters breathlessly. She wears shoes like Di and carries a small brown paper bag. She now sounds like a seasoned Londoner, but is much better spoken than her friend Di

Di Hi. What d'you get?
Brenda Woodbines and Penguins. God Di, it must be great having your own flat. Smoking and playing music whenever you feel like it.

Di lights two cigarettes, passes one to Brenda

Di I keep telling you, Bren. Leave home and we'll get a nice place together. We could have a look in Chelsea. You get a lot of writers living in Chelsea. They sit about in coffee bars, discussing and that.
Brenda Oh, I couldn't Di. My Mum would take it personally. I'd have to leave the country if I left home.
Di (*posing*) How do the shoes look?
Brenda Fab.

Di starts the record again and the two line up. They hold their hands in front of them, in the manner of a dog begging. Di performs the step and Brenda picks it up. They continue to dance as they chat

Di ... and front and over and back and over ... I don't know how you stick it at your place, the way your Dad carries on.

Brenda As it happens, he's not so bad lately. You know he's always sort of lived apart from us and spent most of his time in bed? Well now he's sick so he really *has* to be in bed. Terrible smokers' cough. He hardly ever comes out of his room these days. If he's got something to say to me he says it through Mom. I just wish he'd close his bedroom door, but he can't bear to miss anything.

Di Pity he doesn't croak and give everybody a bit of peace.

Brenda (*a bit shocked*) Di! (*She pauses*) He's got this weird thing about dressing gowns. My Aunty Peace has moved in permanently now and every time one of us walks by Dad's door in a gown, he shouts "*Hoor. Hoor*".

Di What's "*hoor*" mean?

Brenda It's Irish for slag.

Di reacts with indignation

Show us that other one again, the one with the kick.

Di (*dancing*) Kick off your shoe, kick off your shoe, kick off your shoe, kick off your shoe. How does he get on with your little brother?

Brenda (*warmly*) Oh, everyone loves Ted, even my Dad. They get on great, playing cards and that.

Di Change the leg. Change the leg. Change the leg. Change the leg. Any news about your book?

Brenda No. But that's only eight publishers. There's loads more.

Di and Brenda commence a round of handjive

Di Don't get your hopes up, Bren. They don't publish books by girls like us. It's only debs and university girls that get books published. You want to settle down to real life, mate. (*She switches to a routine that features two steps forward followed by two pecking motions of the head, and wing-like movements of the elbows*) Wings, wings, wings wing, Step step, peck peck. Step step, peck peck. Wings, wings, wings, wings.

Brenda (*while stepping and pecking*) No, Di. There must be more to life than working in an office all week and dancing at St Anne's Hall on Saturdays.

Di (*annoyed*) That's exactly why we've started going up West, to the Whisky-A-Go-Go, right?

Di continues dancing while Brenda flops down on the chair

Brenda Do you think he'll be there again tonight, Di? I think he's great, really fab.

Di He's all right, but ...

Brenda But what?

Di He's not our sort Bren, the way he dresses and speaks and that. Didn't you hear him at the bar last week. (*She affects a rather old world English accent*) "Half a pint of mild, if I may. Many thanks." The barman thought he was being sarcastic!

Brenda (*dreamily*) I love the way he speaks. I bet he's from abroad. He has the air of a foreign place on him.

Di *Hot* air, if you want my opinion. I wouldn't be a bit surprised if he turned out to be a five-to-two.

Brenda So what if he is? What's wrong with being Jewish?

Di You'll be wasting your time, that's what's wrong. Their marriages are arranged before they're born, like the Hindus.

Brenda Don't be daft. Anyway, there's a lot I'm gonna do before I get married. But he's so sort of calm looking. Like the man in that advertisement for Erinmore Tobacco. Calm and good tempered.

Brenda goes dreamy and Di gives her a pitying look. The music switches to big volume speakers and the bedsit becomes the Whisky-A-Go-Go. A mirror ball establishes a dance hall mood

Brenda and Di whoop excitedly and strike their set

Mark, aged twenty-four, enters with the whole cast, in sixties outfits. They form two lines and dance The Madison with great energy

Brenda and Di enter and join in

Mark and Brenda steal glances at each other. Brenda nudges Di. Mark positions himself between Brenda and Di. Di is annoyed and dances herself next to Brenda again

The courtship of Brenda and Mark takes place within the choreography of The Madison

The actors playing Bridie and Desmond exit as if tired

Suddenly Di finds herself left out of a formation. She goes to Brenda and pokes at her angrily. Brenda ignores her, already completely involved with Mark

Di flounces off huffily

Brenda and Mark don't notice her go. The music fades and they stroll off, arms around each other

Bridie and Desmond enter with the London flat furniture

The music continues as if heard on Bridie's small radio, in the next scene

SCENE 5

1962. The Engagement Scene. The London flat

Desmond, aged fifty-three, is reading in bed. Bridie, aged fifty-one, in day clothes, is listening to The Madison and knitting a long yellow scarf. The number ends and she turns off the radio

*Brenda, aged twenty-one, enters carrying a bunch of flowers. She creeps up
behind Bridie and puts the flowers under her nose*

Brenda (*warmly*) Hi, Mum.
Bridie (*without looking up*) What's wrong?
Brenda What do you mean, "what's wrong". I bring you a bunch of flowers
and you say "what's wrong". Honestly Mum—I don't know why you're
always so suspicious!

*Bridie smiles knowingly and inspects her knitting. Desmond begins to pay
attention*

Bridie Only another few rows, thank God. I thought this yellow was lovely
in the light of the shop. But sure 'tis sickening in the light here. (*She gets
up and drapes the scarf around Brenda, placing the ball of wool on her head*)
Will I make you a hat to match or would they think you were an egg yolk
on legs? Arra no, the scarf will do on its own.
Brenda Mum ... have you ever thought of visiting a place so warm and
sunny that you wouldn't even *need* a scarf? A place where the air is filled
with the smell of flowers, and cigarettes are only one and six for twenty.

Desmond perks up. All interest

Bridie Am I about to hear something that'll upset me?
Brenda There you go again Mum! Listen: I've been going out with this
really fabulous bloke from Rhodesia. His name is Mark, he's been in
London to study public relations and now that he's qualified he's asked
me to go back with him.
Bridie Are you going this evening or tomorrow morning. I'm only asking so
I can cook accordingly.
Brenda Mum. *Please.*
Bridie What's the snag, Brenda?

Desmond listens intently

Brenda (*airily*) There's no snag—unless it would bother you that he's not
actually a Catholic, as such. He's from a very religious family though—
except for his Uncle, who married an atheist. They're ever so happy—like
Romeo and Juliet, Mark says. And so will we be. We're going to have a
really normal life and never fight, or raise our voices in anger—never!
Bridie (*putting her knitting away firmly*) How long have you known this
character?
Brenda About four months. I'd have told you before but he only proposed
to me last night.
Bridie (*incredulously*) Proposed! Then you're serious about this, when I,
your *mother*, haven't even met him!
Brenda Of course you'll meet him. But I can't very well bring him here. (*She
indicates Desmond with her head*)

Desmond reacts

44   Same Old Moon

When the time is right, Mark says we'll sail home and have a wonderful family get-together. You'll love Mark, Mum. I know you will.
Bridie Well. Let's hear the worst and get it over with. Is he Church of England?
Brenda Noooo.
Bridie Presbyterian?
Brenda No.
Bridie Anglican?
Brenda No.
Bridie Methodist?
Brenda No.
Bridie Baptist?
Brenda No.
Bridie Sure that's about it, unless ... he's not a Jehovah's Witness that wouldn't have a blood transfusion and he white as a sheet?
Brenda He's Jewish, Mum.

Desmond is thrilled, anticipating the explosion to come

Bridie (*slowly and powerfully*) Over my. Dead. Body. Put it out of your head now and we'll say no more about it.
Brenda There's no point in us falling out over this, Mum. I'm going and you can't stop me.
Bridie That's what you think. I can't believe you planned all this behind my back. You sly little rip. *Over my dead body!*

Peace enters

Desmond is ecstatic

Peace What in God's name is going on and the English listening above and below.
Bridie (*distraught*) She's marrying a Jew and going to live among the blacks and atheists out in Africa.
Peace My back's gone. Jesus, Mary and Joseph, my back's gone. (*She stiffens*)
Bridie Are you satisfied—and your aunt in failing health.

Bridie carefully ushers Peace off

Peace (*as she goes*) It's agony, Bridie. Unbearable agony.
Bridie (*as she goes*) Offer it up, Peace. And lie flat–you'll be better lying flat.
Brenda (*whirling around romantically*) I'm twenty one! You can't stop me! I love him, I love him, I love him.

Brenda whirls off

Desmond bounces childishly

Brenda's declarations of love are repeated on an echoing tape, interrupted by a lengthy blast from a ship's horn. The furniture remains on stage

SCENE 6

1962. Outward Bound. On board a ship. A starry sky with a beautiful new moon

We hear water lapping, seagulls

Brenda, aged twenty-one, and Mark, aged twenty-four, perhaps seen in silhouette, chins up like pioneers, enter and appear to sail across a shimmering sea from UR *to* UL

SCENE 7

1965. The Peaceful Scene. Desmond's room in the London flat

Desmond, aged fifty-five, is sitting up in bed, reading a book. Bridie enters with an Electrolux vacuum cleaner and duster

Bridie First Monday of the month!

Desmond (*still reading*) Meaning?

Bridie Now Desmond. You agreed to let me do your room once a month. Look at the state of it and the district nurse due tomorrow. (*She looks under the bed*) Fluff balls as big as grapefruit.

Desmond Not today. I'm not in the mood. Try again in a week and we'll see.

Bridie Why don't you pop into the sitting room for a hour. The doctor said you should walk around a bit. You won't be disturbed. Ted's tinkering with his motorbike, Peace is having her hair permed and Brenda's eight thousand miles away.

Desmond I'm perfectly happy where I am. Subject closed.

Bridie (*dusting a bit*) Is that it for the rest of our lives then? You in here and me in there?

Desmond I'm a sick man, in case you haven't noticed. I can hardly get my breath.

Bridie You've plenty of breath for chatting to strangers on the phone when it suits you.

Desmond Are you jealous?

Bridie Jealous my eye! I just don't want to be living like a widow when I've a husband, large as life.

Desmond You'll be heartbroken when I'm gone, will you?

Bridie ignores this and proceeds with some light cleaning. After a moment, Desmond puts down his book, decides he's in the mood for a chat

Did I ever tell you about the time I hi-jacked a bus? Three of us, I suppose we were seventeen or so, hijacked a double decker bus from the, ah—

Bridie (*cleaning away*) Terminus. The Mount Street Terminus.

Desmond We chose a route and off we went—real devils! When the passengers got on at the bus stop, we asked their destination and told them the fare: "A gumdrop, Missus, or two eggs. A biscuit to go to Ball's Bridge" I've never had such gas.

Bridie smiles, enjoying the story although she's often heard it before

We took everyone right to their doorstep—they thought it was bloody Christmas. "Sure it's the new Tramway's policy to be more obliging, Missus," says I to an ould one with two big shopping bags. (*His tone becomes wistful*) I've never had such gas.

Noticing the sadness in his voice, Bridie stops dusting

Bridie Tell you what: I'll put on the fire and we'll have tea and toast in the sitting room. Just the two of us.

Desmond (*mimicking her scornfully*) "Just the two of us".

Bridie What about it? . . . . . . R.S.V.P.

Desmond Look, I'll meet you half-way. Make the tea and toast and we'll have it in here.

Bridie (*almost flirting*) How do I know I'll be welcome?

Desmond (*getting angry*) Haven't I just asked you! Are you waiting for a gilt-edged invitation!

Pleased, Bridie leaves Desmond's room. She stops outside to fiddle with the cord of the vacuum cleaner

Desmond puts down his book and looks after her. After a pause, he begins to sing softly to himself

(*Singing*)   "Darling you are growing ohhh-old
                      Silver threads among the gold. . ."

Desmond's voice tails off distantly. Outside his room Bridie softly sings another section of the song

Bridie (*singing*)   "Love is always young and fair
                                 What to us is silver hair."

After a moment, Desmond returns to his book

   Bridie exits with her vacuum cleaner

The furniture remains on stage

We hear a ship's horn

SCENE 8

1968. Homeward Bound. On board a ship as Scene 6

Brenda, aged twenty-six, and Mark twenty-eight, return home, sailing from UL *to* UR

SCENE 9

1968. Mark's Scene. Desmond's room in the London flat

Desmond, aged fifty-eight, is sitting up in bed. He looks unwell. There's a knock and he perks up expectantly

Desmond (*warm and friendly*) Just a minute! (*He pats his hair, lights a cigarette*). Come in. In you come. In you come.

Brenda, aged twenty-six, and Mark, aged twenty-eight, enter

Brenda Hello Dad.

Desmond Hello Bren. Lookit how brown you are! And is this himself?

Brenda This is my husband Mark. Mark, this is my Dad.

Mark (*extending his hand*) How do you do, sir.

Desmond (*shaking hands vigorously*) 'Sur' is it? You sound like a real ould colonial and no mistake. Well. I'm sorry I wasn't at the wedding. I hear ye'd a great do out there.

Brenda Mostly friends of Mark's Uncle Tevia. They're quite a clan.

Desmond (*all innocence*) And they like to stick together. They're the same over here and the same in Ireland. Tell me now Bren, did you not feel strange among them all, or have you picked up the lingo?

Brenda and Mark exchange glances

Brenda What lingo?

Mark I think your Dad means Yiddish, darling. Unfortunately, Mr Barnes, it's dying out with the older generation, so there isn't a lot for Brenda to pick up.

Desmond (*feigning intense interest*) Is that so? Sure I never knew that, old ejit that I am. Well hasn't he a lovely turn of phrase Bren, and he so young. (*To Mark*) Was there no *ham* at the wedding so?

Desmond laughs. Mark and Brenda join in nervously, but stop when Desmond's laughter ends in a fit of coughing

Mark I'm sorry you haven't been well, Mr Barnes. Rotten luck.

Desmond (*imitating a plummy doctor*) "Your lungs are in bad shape" says the quack in his English accent. Sure you'd think some of them were being strangled the way they speak. "Caused by smoking sixty a day. It can gallop or creep," says he, "the rate of progress is up to you." (*He maintains the accent*) Bridie, says I—and he still at the door—bring an ashtray and matches in here please. (*He drops the accent*) Anyway, I'd a great youth, so I'm not complaining. Are you fond of a jar, Mark?

Mark I like a cold beer from time to time. And of course we're great wine lovers in Rhodesia.

Desmond Wines, is it? And I was imagining the two of yous knocking 'em back in the tropics. I'd a vision of you sitting on a wooden verandah— yourself in a pair of khaki shorts, a shirt with apertures for a row of bullets in it, and a hat with a leopard-skin band.

Desmond warms to his vision, Brenda looks suspicious

Herself inside in the kitchen, giving orders to the natives. Mosquitoes the size of Tiger Moths buzzing around your heads. (*He waves his arms*) The

drums thumping away (*he drums*) as the sun sets and the two of yous
pissed day and night from the gin and tonics.

Mark and Brenda laugh indulgently

Sure wine is a queer's drink. Ask your mother to bring us in a few
sandwiches, Brenda. I'm sure your man here is starving hungry.
Brenda But Mum's made a special meal, Dad—
Desmond (*ominously*) Are you deaf?
Mark (*winking at Brenda*) I wouldn't mind a snack, darling ...

   Brenda shrugs and exits reluctantly

Desmond smiles at Mark. Mark sits

Mr Barnes, may I just say again how sorry I am that we couldn't be with
you and Mrs Barnes when Ted died.

*Desmond's face hardens for a moment, then he nods, seems grateful for the
sympathy. Mark clears his throat and moves into his prepared speech*

I'd also like to say, for what it's worth, that whilst I understand perfectly
that I could never replace Ted, I'd consider it a privilege to be your
surrogate son, as it were. It would certainly make Brenda happy, poor
darling.
Desmond Thank you, Mark. You seem like a nice boy. I hope "darling"
hasn't been pulling the wool over your eyes ...
Mark (*slapping Desmond's back easily*) No, sir. Now that I've met the
family I reckon I know all there is to know, more or less.
Desmond You fucking well don't, that's the sad part of it, you poor ejit.

Mark speedily withdraws his hand

Mark (*with calm logic*) All the same, we've been married for five years now
and we're very happy. One can't ask for more than that.
Desmond (*exploring a new angle*) I believe ye even have television out there?
Mark (*confused*) Sorry? Oh, *television*. Yes indeed. The service is quite good
actually.
Desmond (*after a pause*) The Jews are running the BBC entirely now, of
course.
Mark (*carefully*) Is that a fact?
Desmond Don't argue with me, whatever-your-name-is. I bloody well know
what I'm talking about. They're running the whole of Britain, as far as
I'm concerned. Banks, shops, industry, the lot!
Mark (*unnerved*) Yes ... well ... uh ...
Desmond "Yes. Well. Uh". Is that the best you can do? Sitting on *my* chair,
married to *my* daughter, living off *my* generosity! I suppose you thought
you'd be on Easy Street here, having one of your holidays at my expense!
Mark (*with smiling logic*) I've only been in the country an hour and a half,
Mr Barnes. I hardly think—
Desmond (*totally enraged*) Listen you: You're not wanted here with your
Mazookas and *Ringlets*! I was going to be nice to you out of pity for the

way that one got you to marry her—but I can see now you deserve each other.

Desmond stubs out his cigarette and struggles to climb out of bed. Mark stands and backs away nervously

Mark Perhaps I should see if the ladies need help with lunch—
Desmond Out, you little runt!

Desmond looks for a weapon, seizes the chair, threatens Mark with it. Mark makes a last attempt to reverse the situation

Mark Mr Barnes, be reasonable . . .
Desmond I'll give you reasonable, by God. I'll give you surrogate son! Out, OUT!

Mark exits hastily

(*Calling after him*) And be sure to take your HOOR with you!

Desmond leans on the chair, a bent and pathetic figure. He slowly returns to his bed, climbs into it. He stares into space

(*In a small, despairing voice*) Ted? . . . (*then louder, anguished*) . . . Ted! . . .
We hear a sad passage of the theme music

SCENE 10

1976. The Hospital Scene. Desmond, aged sixty-six, is in the bed, as last scene

A Nurse enters with an oxygen trolley. She removes the bedspread, revealing a hospital one underneath, crisply tucked in, and a medical chart

Nurse Mr Barnes, you've got a visitor. Let's sit you up a bit. There you are, all comfy? And here's your buzzer, if you need me.

The Nurse exits

Brenda enters. She wears dark court shoes, a raincoat. She carries a small bunch of flowers

Brenda Are you awake, Dad?
Desmond What are you doing here?
Brenda Oh, just passing through.
Desmond Jesus, they must be expecting me to depart sooner than I thought. Did your mother send for you?
Brenda Of course not. I come every few years as you well know.
Desmond Not to see yours truly, you don't.
Brenda How are you feeling?
Desmond If they don't loosen the sheets at the foot of the bed, my feet will go gang-gur-een. It's bloody awful in this place, full of foreigners in turbans. So. You're still married to that fella.

Brenda loosens the sheets, then sits on a chair at the head of the bed, facing D

Brenda Yep! Twelfth anniversary coming up. Mark and I are very happy. We did well to move to Australia when we did. He's manager of a big promotions company now. We've got a beautiful home, nice friends and everything.

Desmond 'Twon't last though. Well, it's obvious 'twon't last. A dull fella like that. Sure I've more personality in my little finger than all your boy friends put together.

Brenda You never met any of my boy friends.

Desmond Sure I didn't have to meet them to know the kind they'd be: Dull fellas one and all. Predictable as the sun going down at night, and *faces* on them that would remind a person of . . . of . . . a dose of Milk of Magnesia!

Brenda (*smiling*) What type would you have picked out for me then?

Desmond Aren't you very chatty, all of a sudden? And nothing except a few postcards for years. (*He waggles his head scornfully*) "Bali" Big Deal. (*He sings*) "Bali Hiiiii". You're lucky the pair of ye didn't catch leprosy. Anyway, I'd be a liar if I said I missed you. I didn't, and that's all about it.

Brenda (*determinedly cheerful*) I'm getting quite a reputation as a writer, Dad. Mostly short stories and articles. I think you'd be surprised.

Desmond Why would I? If you've any talent it's thanks to my genes, so you needn't be puffing yourself up.

Brenda (*after a pause*) Dad, do you think we could just sort of . . . forget the past? I'd like to feel that—

Desmond (*cutting in quickly*) This is the place where his nibs Douglas Bader had his wooden legs screwed on. They've his plaque stuck up in the entrance hall.

Brenda Oh, of course. The war hero.

Desmond They used his life story in *Reach For The Sky*. One of the best films ever made. That, and *The Bridge Over The River Kwai*. (*Pause*) And *The Wages of Fear*. That was a good one. French, but it had a proper story to it.

Brenda (*after a pause*) Can I ask you something, Dad? Is it because I wasn't a boy? I mean is that the reason you never liked me?

Desmond (*very uncomfortable*) I thought we were going to forget the past?

Brenda (*coaxingly*) Come on, Dad . . .

Desmond (*irritably*) If I didn't like you it was because you were too much like myself. People never like people like themselves. They get on their nerves, reading each other's minds and so on. Wouldn't any gom know that!

Brenda But *how* am I like you?

Desmond (*angrily*) The way you always think there's something better over the next bloody hill. Rhodeeesia! Austraaalia! It's the same old moon shining down wherever you are. Listen: You were brought up to look out for yourself and the parent who gives his children the gift of independence is worth ten fools who'd be falling over themselves to make pals of their kids.

Brenda looks sad. Desmond softens slightly

One thing I like about you is that you never give up—even when things get rough. That's all I'm going to say. Don't expect me to turn into Spencer Tracy just because I'm dying.

Brenda (*distressed*) You're not dying.

Desmond Don't argue with me. Look. I'll give you a bit of advice for what it's worth: If you want to amount to anything, never be slopping around in a dressing gown. 'Twas dressing gowns that ruined things between me and your mother. Before she had you she was as fresh as a daisy, up and washed and dressed early in the morning. Neat as a new pin when I'd come home from work. And then she moved into her dressing gown period. The dressing gown is the world's most demoralising garment, because people who go round in dressing gowns look as if they've given up hope. There y' are now Brenda. Some fatherly advice before they nail me down.

Brenda Dad—

Brenda moves as if to embrace Desmond. He panics, presses the buzzer frantically

The Nurse runs in and places the oxygen mask over Desmond's mouth and nose

Nurse Heavens. Mr Barnes, you shouldn't have let her tire you out like this. (*To Brenda*) I'm afraid I'll have to ask you to leave, you've quite worn him out, he needs rest.

Brenda I'm sorry. (*She moves towards the exit reluctantly*)

The Nurse gestures for Brenda to keep moving

Brenda exits

Desmond pushes away the oxygen mask

Desmond (*urgently*) Run after my daughter, Nurse and tell her . . . tell her I said . . . tell her I said she looks nice.

Nurse (*putting the mask back*) I will. Or you can tell her yourself next time, Mr Barnes. Just relax now. Close your eyes and take it easy. Thaaat's better. That's muuuch better.

The Mozart theme is heard as the Lights fade and the Nurse pushes off Desmond's bed

When the stage is clear, Brenda enters

She is dressed as in Scene 1. But without her 80s jacket and shoes, which have been in view throughout the play, near the stool. Brenda moves slowly and thoughtfully

She goes to the stool, where she changes her shoes and slips on her jacket. She takes her fur coat from the wings and puts it on. She picks up her briefcase and exits, still moving slowly

We hear a Christmas carol as if played on a radio

The actors for the last scene bring on their furniture

SCENE 11

1980s. The Last Scene. The flat. Late afternoon

A radio softly plays a carol, and the rosy glow from a small electric heater faces u. There's a tiny artificial Christmas tree, adorned with fairy lights, which are switched on. Bridie, aged sixty-six, in yet another gown, is dozing on the sofa, a rug over her knees. The ghost of Desmond dozes in his room

Peace, aged sixty-two, enters stealthily, also in another gown. She is wearing a foam rubber neck brace. She switches off the fairy lights, the heater, and finally the radio. She begins to sneak off again

Bridie (*still apparently asleep*) Put them back on.
Peace (*plaintively*) What for and you asleep? Sure there's money being thrown down the drain in this house. I've just turned off the immersion heater. It was *boiling*, ready to explode!
Bridie Put it back on, Brenda will want a bath.
Peace Put *everything* on so, if we've money to burn!

Peace switches the radio on very loudly, then the heater, and Christmas tree. Bridie gets up and calmly turns off the radio

Bridie As long as our pensions are index-linked we can afford a few luxuries. (*She yawns*). Are you sure that Christmas tree doesn't look common? Calm down now and put the kettle on.
Peace (*sarcastically*) I'll fill it to the brim, will I, for fear of missing a chance to waste electricity!

Peace exits, moving strangely because of her brace. When she's safely off, Bridie imitates her movements and makes a face behind her back. She then shakes out and folds the knee-rug

Bridie (*to the audience*) Sometimes I wish his nibs were alive to throw her out.

Desmond is lit

The two of them had fights that would make your hair stand on end.

Desmond smiles modestly

I'll never forget the night he flung all her clothes out the window, and the wind howling. We retrieved some, some were stolen and a dress got caught in the branches of a tree. It flapped away up there the whole winter, till there was nothing left but a few old rags, waving in the breeze. No. I can't say I want him back, but he was useful for keeping *certain people* under control.

Brenda enters and notices the Christmas tree

Brenda Hi Mum. That's nice.
Bridie Isn't it great? All we had to do was unfold it from last year. Lights and all, still on the branches.

Brenda smiles and sits down wearily

Well? What did the "agent" say. The great Bunty.

Brenda Her name's Bonny.

Bridie Bonny, Binny, Banny. What did she say?

Brenda (*very carefully*) She said she didn't feel she could represent me after all. Her heart wouldn't be in it, because her heart is already divided up among the clients she represents now. She said success in Australia doesn't count because Australian audiences aren't all that fussy. She said my little one-act was quite sweet but that she hadn't felt obliged to read beyond scene one of my comedy, because one doesn't have to eat a whole egg to know that it's rotten.

A silence falls. Bridie leans over and pats Brenda's hand.

Bridie (*sympathetically*) Well, I suppose a one like that would know her onions.

Brenda That's right.

There's another little silence

Bridie Peace won't be long with the tea.

Brenda Mum, it's all over between me and Mark. He's living with somebody else now. So I'd like to stay here for a while.

Bridie (*briskly*) Now if you'd told me that in the first place, I'd have let Peace keep her room and put you in your father's room. Peace? *Peace!* Will you bring in the tea before we forget we were thirsty.

Peace enters, pushing the trolley

I've great news for you: Brenda's home for good!

Peace (*equally briskly*) She can have Desmond's room so, instead of keeping it like a shrine.

Desmond reacts

Now, how many sugars did you say?

Brenda (*after a pause*) One and a half.

Peace (*not believing her ears*) But black?

Brenda With milk, please.

Desmond sinks down in the bed. Peace hums Jingle Bells *cheerfully and continues with the tea pouring. Bridie suddenly jumps up*

Bridie Wait! Wait a minute now before we get too settled.

Bridie exits

Peace beams at Brenda. Brenda manages a faint response

(*Off*) Close your eyes and open your hands.

Brenda complies

Bridie enters bearing a parcel wrapped with Christmas paper

Now: an early Christmas from myself and your Aunty Peace.

Brenda removes the wrapping, assisted by Bridie and advised by Peace

Peace Careful now, love. Don't let the Sellotape tear the paper.

Brenda withdraws from the wrapping a dressing gown exactly like the ones Bridie and Peace are wearing, but in a third colour. When she sees the gown she is transfixed. Desmond is disgusted

Peace and Bridie haul her up and remove her fur coat. Then they dress Brenda in the gown, perkily singing 'We Three Kings' as they button and tie and tug and adjust. They stand back admiringly. Desmond claps his hands to his face, but peeks through his fingers

Bridie Now you're talking.

Brenda sits down in the middle of the sofa. Bridie sits to her left, Peace hands out cups then squashes in to her right. It's a tight squeeze

Bridie ⎱ *(together)* I'll finish that—
Peace ⎰   We'll get no—
Peace *(unusually sweet tempered)* After you, Bridie.
Bridie *(equally charming)* I was going to say that I'll finish that yellow scarf for Brenda. It's still on top of the wardrobe, in my brown suitcase. What were you going to say, dear?
Peace I was just thinking that we'll get no Christmas card from Australia this year. And then I thought of how people put "to all at eight-oh-four" on cards to us.

Pause

Bridie *(with a slight edge)* What about it?
Peace They'll mean Brenda as well, God bless her. From now on, all at eight-oh-four will include Brenda.

All of them consider this. Peace and Bridie smile and nod contentedly, Brenda is expressionless. Moving as one, the three slowly raise their cups to their lips. They sip, pause, sip again. Still carefully synchronised, they lower the cups. All seems lost. They drink again, lower the cups again

The ghost of Desmond sits up and forward, as if willing Brenda to pay attention to him. We hear the distorted theme music, as in Scene 1. Brenda feels Desmond's presence, slowly turns her head towards him. Peace and Bridie sit back, cosy and relaxed

Desmond *(looking at Brenda)* One thing I like about you is that you never give up, even when things get rough.
Brenda *(after a pause)* Just one thing Mum.
Bridie What's that, love?
Brenda I won't be staying long, but while I am here I won't be going to Mass. Not even at Christmas.

Bridie and Peace put their cups down and struggle to rise from the sofa

Bridie This is *my home* and as long as you live in *my home* you'll go to Mass!

Peace My back Bridie, my back! Sacred Heart, I'm finished.

The theme music and the sound of squabbling birds fades in

  Bridie assists Peace off

Bridie (*as she goes*) That's lovely and your Aunt's back destroyed. Now I'll have to put her down.

Peace (*off*) "I wandered lonely as a cloud, that floats on high o'er vales and hills . . ."

Brenda and Desmond watch them go. Brenda puts down her cup, and smiling, begins to unbutton the gown in a very businesslike way. She stands, slips off the gown, rolls it into a ball. The end music begins to build as she turns to the approving ghost of Desmond

After a little pause, Brenda smiles and flings the gown high, high into the air

There's a snap Black-out before the gown falls

FURNITURE AND PROPERTY LIST

PROLOGUE

(Seen and used throughout the play)

On stage: Low stool. *On it:* school exercise book
Statue of the Virgin Mary
Teddy bear or doll
Brown school sandals
White socks

Off stage: Suitcase, briefcase, fur coat **(Brenda)**

ACT I

SCENE 1

On stage: *Living room*
Small two-seater sofa
End table. *On it:* radio
Easy chair

Bedroom
Bed. *On it:* a woven bedspread
Night-table. *On it:* tumbler

Off stage: Gilded tea trolley **(Bridie)**
Suitcase, fur coat, briefcase. *In it:* press clippings in plastic sleeves **(Brenda)**
Milk jug **(Bridie)**
Sugar bowl **(Bridie)**
Cups, saucers, spoons **(Bridie)**

Personal: **Peace:** spectacles (one pair on, one on her person)
Bridie: spectacles (on her person)
Brenda: wristwatch
Desmond: newspaper

SCENE 2

On stage: Bar counter. *On it:* old-fashioned radio
Barstools or chairs
Shelves behind bar. *On them:* bottles of liquor, various glasses

SCENE 3

Strike: Pub set

Re-set: Bed
Night-table

Set: Tall stool, box of chocolates
On bed: candlewick bedspread, smouldered sheet (hidden)
On night-table: bottle of whiskey, glass, cigarettes (non-filtered), matches,
    ashtray

<h2 style="text-align:center">SCENE 4</h2>

Strike: Bedroom setting

Set: Statue of the Virgin Mary
Stool

Personal: **Mother Superior:** Biscuit tin. *In it:* boudoir biscuit, doughnut

<h2 style="text-align:center">SCENE 5</h2>

Set: Bed. *On it:* patchwork bedspread, **Peace'**s knitting
Night-table. *On it:* glass
Wardrobe with mirror. *Inside it:* religious picture, red light

Personal: **Bella:** headscarf
Brenda: notebook and pencil
Priest: cigarettes and matches
Granny: various layers of clothing/undergarments at the director's dis-
    cretion, false teeth

<h2 style="text-align:center">SCENE 6</h2>

Strike: Set for Scene 5

Set: Café Daphne's trolley. *On it:* tea urn, baking utensils, tin of coconut, tarts,
    cup, saucer, spoon, menu, pencil, string bag, notebook

Offstage: Note **(Brenda)**
Artificial flower **(Caruso)**

<h2 style="text-align:center">SCENE 7</h2>

On stage: Upholstered wing-backed chair
Long wooden bench
Hanging laundry rack
Religious picture set above and behind chair

Personal: **Michael:** mail satchel. *In it:* Letters, particularly one airmail stickered, and
    red-sealed *In it:* large gold medallion on a fine chain
Granny: walking stick
Brenda: skipping rope

<h2 style="text-align:center">SCENE 8</h2>

On stage: Section of wall (possibly ivy-covered)

Off stage: Skipping rope **(Brenda)**
Bicycle **(Kevin)**

Personal: **Kevin:** cap

ACT II

SCENE 1

On stage: Large old-fashioned pram laden with parcels, enamel teapot etc.

Off stage: Suitcases **(Bridie)**
Various parcels **(Bridie)**
Baby bottle **(Bridie)**

Personal: **Brenda:** Teddy bear, statue of the Madonna
Mrs Geeny: clipboard, pen
Mrs Brown; clipboard, pen

SCENE 2

On stage: Coronation bunting
Crate

Off stage: Stilts **(Di)**
Stilts **(Trevor)**

Personal: **Brenda:** notebook, pen

SCENE 3

Strike: Bunting and crate

Off stage: Tartan rug, picnic basket. *In it:* two wrapped greaseproof packets, flask,
pencil, notebook, two plastic cups, teacloth **(Brenda)**

Personal: **Desmond:** Binoculars, race card

SCENE 4

On stage: Pink chest of drawers. *On it:* Record player. *On the turntable;* 78 record
Lamp, draped with a red cloth. *In it:* items of clothing
Chair

Off stage: Small brown paper bag. *In it:* cigarettes (Woodbines), matches, biscuits
(Penguins)—not seen **(Brenda)**

SCENE 5

Strike: Record player
Lamp
Cushions

Re-set:
Bed

Set: Small two-seater sofa
End table. *On it:* radio
Easy chair

On bed: woven bedspread
Night-table.

Off stage: Bouquet of flowers **(Brenda)**

Personal: Knitting—4 ft Scarf in progress **(Bridie)**
            Newspaper **(Desmond)**

SCENE 6

Section of ship's rail. Lifebuoy

SCENE 7

As Scene 5

Off stage: Vacuum cleaner and duster **(Bridie)**

Personal: **Desmond:** book

SCENE 8

As Scene 6

SCENE 9

As Scene 5

Personal: **Desmond:** cigarettes and matches

SCENE 10

Set: *On bed:* white bedspread under woven one
             Pillows
             Medical chart
             Chair

Off stage: *Buzzer on cord.* Oxygen trolley with mask **(Nurse)**
             Bouquet of flowers **(Brenda)**

Strike·   Medical chart
             Oxygen trolley
             Buzzer

SCENE 11

As Scene 5

Set: *On bed:* woven bedspread
             Knee rug
             Electric heater
             Tiny artificial Christmas tree. *On it:* Fairy lights

Off stage: Tea trolley. *On it:* tea pot, three cups and saucers, milk jug, sugar bowl,
                 spoons **(Peace)**
             Parcel in Christmas paper. *In it:* dressing gown **(Bridie)**

Personal: Neck brace **(Peace)**

LIGHTING PLOT

Practical fittings required: Christmas tree lights for Act II.

Various interior and exterior settings

ACT I

To open: Overall general lighting

Cue 1	**Brenda** exits slowly *Crossfade to Scene 1 interior lighting. Dim light on bedroom area*	(Page *xi*)
Cue 2	**Bridie:** "... like his meat underdone." *Lights up on Desmond*	(Page 4)
Cue 3	**Brenda** stops on threshold of bedroom *Living room lights dim*	(Page 7)
Cue 4	**Brenda** returns to the others and sits *Living room lights up again*	(Page 8)
Cue 5	**Brenda** exits *Light on **Desmond** fades*	(Page 8)
Cue 6	**Peace** exits with the trolley *Crossfade to Scene 3*	(Page 9)
Cue 7	**Brenda** begins to sway *Lighting effect of train*	(Page 13)
Cue 8	**Brenda** pushes the bed off *Crossfade to Scene 4*	(Page 14)
Cue 9	Scene change music *Crossfade to Scene 5*	(Page 16)
Cue 10	**Brenda** "It is, Granny." *Fade up special spot on Granny*	(Page 20)
Cue 11	**Granny** delivers a hearty snore *Fade up rosy lighting and mirror ball effect*	(Page 20)
Cue 12	**Brenda;** "Oh, bless me, Father ..." *Bring up full lights*	(Page 21)
Cue 13	**Peace** pushes off the wardrobe *Crossfade to Scene 6*	(Page 21)
Cue 14	**Brenda** exits sadly *Crossfade to Scene 7*	(Page 25)
Cue 15	**Granny:** "Our prayers have been answered!" *Crossfade to Scene 8*	(Page 30)

Cue 16	Orchestral version of "Danny Boy" plays *Slow fade to Black-out*	(Page 32)

ACT II

To open: General effect of late afternoon light

Cue 17	We hear the squeak of a door being opened *Snap on a shaft of light*	(Page 34)
Cue 18	**Bridie** and **Brenda** walk off *Crossfade to Scene 2*	(Page 35)
Cue 19	To open Scene 2 *General effect of afternoon light*	(Page 35)
Cue 20	Huge clap of thunder *Lengthy flash of lightning*	(Page 37)
Cue 21	**Brenda** gives a shaky little wave towards heaven *Crossfade to Scene 3*	(Page 37)
Cue 22	**Brenda** follows **Desmond** *Crossfade to Scene 4*	(Page 40)
Cue 23	The music increases in volume *Fade lights; bring up mirror ball effect*	(Page 40)
Cue 24	**Brenda** and **Mark** stroll off *Crossfade to Scene 5*	(Page 42)
Cue 25	**Desmond** bounces childishly *Crossfade to exterior lighting for Scene 6*	(Page 44)
Cue 26	**Brenda** and **Mark** 'sail' across stage *Crossfade to Scene 7*	(Page 45)
Cue 27	Ship's horn sounds *Crossfade to Scene 8*	(Page 46)
Cue 28	**Brenda** and **Mark** 'sail' across stage *Crossfade to Scene 9*	(Page 46)
Cue 29	**Desmond:** "Ted? . . . Ted! . . ." *Crossfade to Scene 10*	(Page 49)
Cue 30	To open Scene 10 *General overall lighting*	(Page 49)
Cue 31	**Nurse:** "That's m-u-u-u-ch better." *Bring lights down slowly till the end of Scene*	(Page 51)
Cue 32	To open Scene 11 *General interior lighting. Christmas tree lights are on, rosy glow from electric heater*	(Page 52)
Cue 33	**Peace** switches off Christmas tree and electric heater *Snap off tree and heater lights*	(Page 52)
Cue 34	**Peace** switches on heater and Christmas tree lights *Snap on heater and tree lights*	(Page 52)

Cue 35   **Bridie:** ". . . to throw her out."   (Page 52)
           Light **Desmond**

Cue 36   **Brenda** flings the gown high   (Page 55)
           Snap black-out

EFFECTS PLOT

PROLOGUE

Cue 1   To open   (Page *xi*)
              Prologue and theme music: Mozart's Variations in C Major
              K. 265. Continue throughout scene

ACT I

Cue 2   To open Scene 1   (Page 1)
              Loudly squabbling birds

Cue 3   **Peace:** "... I poison the lot of you!"   (Page 1)
              Fade birds

Cue 4   **Brenda** stops on threshold of bedroom   (Page 7)
              Theme music, faint and distorted

Cue 5   **Brenda** returns to others   (Page 8)
              Cut theme music

Cue 6   **Peace** exits with the trolley   (Page 9)
              40s music plays. Radio static

Cue 7   **Barman** tunes the radio   (Page 9)
              Radio frequencies being flipped through, then pips, then a 1940s-
              style newscast as script p. 9

Cue 8   As bar set is struck   (Page 11)
              Music: Glenn Miller or similar 40s dance music. Cut when ready

Cue 9   **Brenda** tiptoes back to the stool   (Page 12)
              Clock ticking

Cue 10   **Brenda** falls asleep   (Page 13)
              Smoke issues from the bedclothes

Cue 11   **Brenda** wipes her eyes   (Page 13)
              Steam-train whistle

Cue 12   **Brenda** begins to sway as if on board a train   (Page 13)
              Train pulling out of a station and gathering speed

Cue 13   **Brenda** pushes off the bed   (Page 14)
              Fade train effect; bring up schoolgirls' choir. Cut when next scene
              is ready

Cue 14   **Brenda** takes a bite out of the biscuit   (Page 16)
              Scene change music

Cue 15   **Granny** delivers several hearty snores   (Page 20)
              Music: "Limelight" theme music

Cue 16	**Brenda:** "Oh, bless me, Father …" *Cut music*	(Page 21)
Cue 17	**Granny** chases **Brenda** off *Music: lively sequence from theme music*	(Page 21)
Cue 18	**Peace** pushes off wardrobe *Mandolins play, cut when Scene 6 begins*	(Page 21)
Cue 19	During crossfade to Scene 7 *Music: non-vocal version of "Kiss Me, Honey Honey, Kiss Me"*	(Page 25)
Cue 20	**Peace** enters *Fade music during* **Peace***'s opening lines*	(Page 25)
Cue 21	Crossfade to Scene 8 *Merry peal of church bells and music*	(Page 30)
Cue 22	**Brenda** starts skipping *Cut bells and music*	(Page 30)
Cue 23	There's a scream (off) *Small crash—bicycle against dustbin*	(Page 31)
Cue 24	**Brenda:** "Don't, Kevin, don't!" *Big splash—bicycle in canal*	(Page 32)
Cue 25	**Kevin** sings "Danny Boy" *Music: Fade in full orchestral version of "Danny Boy", letting it swell majestically*	(Page 32)

ACT II

Cue 26	To open *Music: "Rule Britannia" (instrumental only)*	(Page 33)
Cue 27	As **Bridie** enters and exits at the opening of the scene *Fade music*	(Page 33)
Cue 28	**Desmond:** "And then her nibs arrived." *Baby cries. Stop when* **Desmond** *coos*	(Page 33)
Cue 29	**Desmond** strides off *Baby gives single wail*	(Page 34)
Cue 30	**Bridie** mimes knocking at a large door *Three echoing knocks, the turning of a massive key and the squeak of a door being opened*	(Page 34)
Cue 31	As **Bridie** exits *Music: "Land of Hope and Glory"*	(Page 35)
Cue 32	Black-out *Cut music*	(Page 35)
Cue 33	Still chanting, **Di** and **Trevor** force **Brenda** to the ground *Huge clap of thunder*	(Page 37)
Cue 34	To open Scene 3 *Race course atmosphere*	(Page 37)

Cue 35 **Brenda:** "... on my birthday, Dad, wouldn't she?"   (Page 39)
          Race and commentary heard in distance

Cue 36 **Di** brings on record player   (Page 40)
          Music: a rather tinny version of "The Madison"

Cue 37 **Brenda** goes dreamy   (Page 42)
          Music: big-volume speakers version of "The Madison"

Cue 38 As **Brenda** and **Mark** stroll off   (Page 42)
          Fade music to a tinny level, as if from a small radio

Cue 39 **Bridie** turns radio off   (Page 42)
          Cut music

Cue 40 **Brenda:** I love him, I love him ..."   (Page 44)
          Brenda'*s voice echoing "I love him", fading to blast on ship's horn*

Cue 41 As Scene 6 begins   (Page 45)
          Bring up sound of gulls, lapping water

Cue 42 **Bridie** exits   (Page 46)
          Ship's horn blows

Cue 43 **Desmond:** "Ted? ... Ted! ..."   (Page 49)
          Music: Mozart theme music. Cut when ready

Cue 44 **Nurse:** "That's m-u-u-ch better"   (Page 51)
          Music: Mozart theme music

Cue 45 **Brenda** exits   (Page 51)
          Christmas carol plays

Cue 46 **Peace** switches the radio off   (Page 52)
          Cut music

Cue 47 **Peace** switches the radio on   (Page 52)
          Music: another Christmas carol, louder

Cue 48 **Bridie** turns the radio off   (Page 52)
          Cut music

Cue 49 **Peace:** "Sacred heart, I'm finished."   (Page 55)
          Music: Mozart theme music; sound of squabbling birds. Continues throughout rest of scene

MADE AND PRINTED IN GREAT BRITAIN BY
LATIMER TREND & COMPANY LTD PLYMOUTH

MADE IN ENGLAND